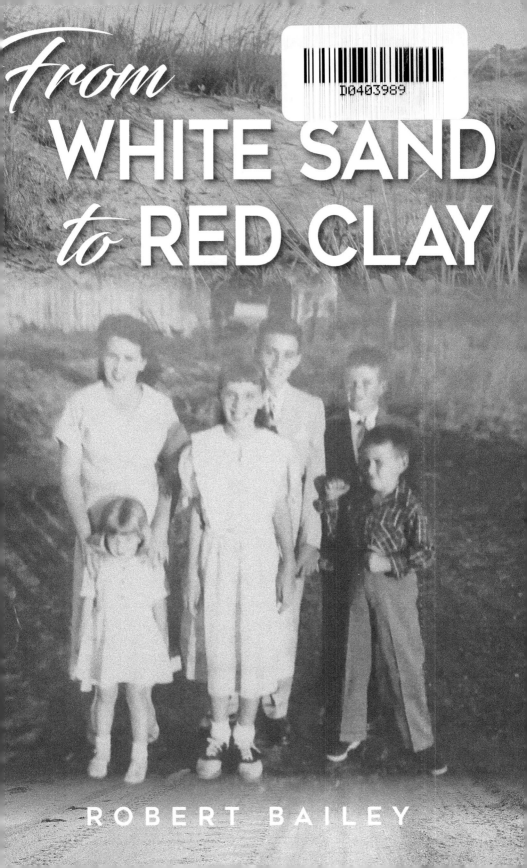

From WHITE SAND *to* RED CLAY

ROBERT BAILEY

Dedication

To my Mama: Love is patient and kind; love does not envy or boast; it is not arrogant or rude. It does not insist on its own way, it is not irritable or resentful, it does not rejoice at wrongdoing, but rejoices with the truth. Love bears all things, believes all things, hopes all things, endures all things. 1 Corinthians 13:4-7

Acknowledgements

I could not agree more with Thomas Jefferson when he said. "The happiest moments of my life have been the few which I have passed at home in the bosom of my family. Thank you Johnny, Jody, Sarah, Darlene and Barbara - yes Barbara, the sister I never knew, who left this world just as I was entering.

To my girlfriend and my wife, Gloria, (yes one in the same) I thank you from the bottom of my eighth-grade romance heart to my quintuple bypassed heart. You have been there. You are as much a sister to my sisters and brothers as I am a brother to them. My mother saw you as her fourth daughter. Your free spirit has been a balance to my stoicism. You danced when no one else heard the music. Your support and encouragement are responsible for the existence of *From White Sand to Red Clay*. I love you.

Special thanks to the team at Palmetto Publishing. Roy, Kristin and Abbey and those working behind the scenes are the best - working through Covid, delays, my abuse of the comma and my lack of computer skills to guide me to a final product.

h

Prologue

My mama's health had been rather uneventful—right up to the end. There were the occasional ingrown toe-nails, a recurrent urinary tract infection, and the ever lasting sensation that she was icy cold. She was forever layered, even in the summer, with thermal undies and a triply jogging suit with a matching knitted toboggan. She had a fall now and again—one that ripped a folded dish-towel sized layer of skin from her knee to her ankle. She seemed oblivious to pain. Gallstones, kidney stones, hernias, and birthing babies were but a distraction.

Mama was a story teller—right up to the end. I don't mean she was a liar—far from it. She was a story teller from her deepest roots—a Blarney-custodian-of-oral tradition kind of storyteller. She was the treasurer of her own biography. As kids, we would gather around the kitchen table to listen to the stories—stories we had heard many times over—stories about the orphanage, the nuns, about Charleston during the Depression, about her mother's sleeping sickness, about the death of a child or two, and her father's love of the grape. She would repeat the tales of the move from the white sands of Sullivan's Island to the red clay hills of northwest Georgia. She was ever ready to repeat a tale when one was requested. "Tell us about the time you …" we would ask. The stories never wavered. There was no embellishment, no change in the script. Yet every time I heard the narrative of Muff and her sister Nora, I would hang on to every word, words I could have likely repeated myself but didn't have the gift of an Irish chronicler.

Mama told stories that were the truth—her truth. But sometimes truth is gossip, a fantasy even, or a fable. However, to the witness of truth, it is grounded in fact. What I tell you here is my honest transcription of my mama's truth. Here, I will let Mama tell her story.

CHARLESTON, SOUTH CAROLINA, 1921–1936

Chapter 1

Muff's Family

My ma and pa came from different bricks of the Charleston cobble-stone streets. My pa was beggared and barren, unwashed and vulgar. My ma, though not affluent, came from Charleston's Irish bourgeoi-sie. My ma's family were first-generation Irish immigrants who worked unrelentingly hard. Her ma's and pa's families pooled their earnings and kept their resolve to rise above their impoverished Irish roots. My ma was one of nine, the baby of a strict Irish Catholic upbringing, with three sisters who were self-designated to guide her through life's odyssey.

All my aunts sniffed their collective noses at my pa. From their porch he was white trash. Maybe he was. My pa's life was not washed in holy water. He held few memories of his own ma and pa. His pa passed in a fishing accident off the coast of Georgetown during a wind storm just months before my pa was born. His ma died when he was only four years old. With the passing of his parents, he was sent to live with his only kin, his grandma Knight.

His grandma Knight ran a boarding house on Cumberland Street in Charleston. She and my pa lived in the side room off from the kitchen. The remainder of the rooms were saved for her paying customers.

The house itself abutted the Bucket of Blood Saloon. Many of the Bucket's patrons and their women friends utilized my great-grandma's boarding house overnight. My pa was the laddie of all the girls who boarded at Great-Grandma Knight's.

While the ladies loved him, my great-grandma Knight found my pa to be a loath-some creature. She was not a loving woman, and my pa suffered from her fits of rage. Her rage lasted for ten years, and he was a lucky boy to be shut of her when her liver hardened enough to kill her.

My pa was ambushed by the polio when he was five years old and remained a cripple for the length of his life. Perhaps that caused some of his bitterness, but if truth be told, it was having to live with Great-Grandma Knight for ten years that really stirred his bile.

When my pa was fourteen years old his grandma Knight finally joined her son and daughter-in-law in paradise, though my pa had his doubts about her settling in the promised land. She was more fit to hold a position of high ranking in the other place—that was his thinking.

My pa calculated being shut of his grandma was a blessing, but there was nothing blessed about what happened to him. Great-Grandma Knight was a needy woman and on city assistance. At her passing the City of Charleston sold her boardinghouse and an adjacent lot to pay for her taxes and personal debts. My pa thought that since she had so many friends in the city departments, those gentlemen would look after her interests, but they didn't. My pa was left with nothing. He had no family and he had no money.

Pa was taken in by Red Robertson and his ma. My pa's friend Red was also a cripple, having been hit by a train a few years earlier when he and my pa were playing on the tracks down at the train yard. Red and my pa, they had one good leg between them.

After about a year Mrs. Robertson said she couldn't take care of two cripples, let alone one. So my pa was out. After that, my pa worked on the shrimp boats at the boat yards in Charleston. The work wasn't steady because most of the ships' captains were superstitious about having a crippled boy on their boats. Any bad haul was blamed on my pa, and he would be fired and sent looking for another captain to take a chance on the shrimper's shaman. If my pa wasn't working on a shrimp boat, he had no place to call home. Most nights he slept in abandoned boats at the ship yard.

As a young man my pa held a number of odd jobs since no shrimp boat captain would hire him a second time. None of his jobs were steady. He was a ship's cook, a blacksmith's apprentice, and a housepainter. He excelled as a house painter. Sometimes he would paint houses just for the room and board. In fact, he was painting houses when he met my ma.

My ma's tender years were not stifled like those of my pa. She was from a money-bagging second-generation Irish Catholic family from Charleston. Grandma O'Kelly, my ma's ma, had come from Ireland in 1870 or so with her three sisters. My Grandpa O'Kelly had come over sometime earlier, during the potato famine. He was a hard worker. He invested his money in cheap housing on the border of Charleston's seedier side, housing that he rented to his relatives and friends in a shameless credit crunch.

Grandpa and Grandma O'Kelly generated four daughters and five sons. My ma's two older sisters, Louise and Bridget, married into Irish money. My ma, whose name was Delia, didn't. She married my pa, Jakey Knight, which was about as far from money as you could get. My ma's other sister, Katie, remained a bachelor girl, but she was still able to turn the dollar.

The fact was, my ma was almost an old maid herself. She was thirty-seven years old when she met my pa during the summer of 1917. My pa was painting my aunt Katie's house. Remember, Katie was the single sister. My ma was boarding with Aunt Katie at this time.

Aunt Katie was a maid at the Charleston Hotel, and while she was at work, my ma and pa became acquainted. They got wedded on the first day of October in that same year. My sister was born the following March. She was named Nora Kate in honor of Aunt Katie, since it was on Aunt Katie's settee that she was conceived.

My ma once told me that she instantly fell in love with my pa. He was shorter than she was by a nose to a forehead, but she said that allowed her to have a better look at his wavy, coal-black hair. Besides, my ma said that she was not much of a looker herself and she felt honored that a fine, handsome man would give her the second eye.

The truth is that my ma was a handsome woman herself, but in an unaffected manner. She was tall and elegant in an athletic sort of way. If she ever dressed up, which she didn't, she could have been accused of being pretty.

All my ma's relatives were angry with her for getting with child and marrying my pa. They thought she was marrying beneath her family, which I guess she was. Why would she marry a crippled, uneducated, alcoholic, generally unemployed house-painter? They all wanted to know.

"Because I have to," she answered them all, never bothering to explain her love for him to them.

So as I said, my sister Nora was born that March in 1918.

My twin and I were born three years later, but my brother died right after he was christened. Joseph was his name. He was called Bubba. That didn't matter, though. His names were buried at the Saint Lawrence Cemetery with him, and neither his name nor he was ever spoken of again by my ma and pa. I came to learn that being born a twin is like having a mirror with you all the time, only my mirror was broken when Bubba died, and the bad luck followed with it.

My given name was Mary Margaret Knight, but my sister Nora christened me "Muffin" because I was such a small baby and because she was three when I was born and didn't want to be bothered with my alliterative title. Sis even found the name Muffin to be an imposition. Muff took less effort, and it seemed more appropriate. When it all settled, I became Muff. I returned the favor and dubbed Nora with the tag "Sister," then "Sissy," and finally "Sis".

Before I was a year old, my ma came down with the sleeping sickness. Of course, I don't remember a lot about my ma's illness, but I have been told that when I was very young, she was in and out of her sleeping spells.

She only stayed in the hospital a short while. There wasn't much they could do for her there. My ma and pa continued to board at Aunt Katie's house. Aunt Katie disapproved of their marriage and bastard child, but not so much that she would give up on potential paying customers. Besides, it allowed all my ma's sisters a chance to keep tabs on my pa. Me and Sis, however, didn't get to stay with ma and pa. Ever since my ma took sick with the sleeping sickness, me and Sis stayed with Aunt Bridget and Aunt Louise. We'd stay one month with Aunt Bridget and then one month with Aunt Louise.

We got to stay at Aunt Katie's with my ma and pa on weekends, if my pa was sober. My pa was sober when he didn't have a job, which was most of the time. If he was employed and he had money, then he would be drunk on weekends, and me and Sis would be detained at our aunts' pleasure.

By the time we reached school age, and as my ma got better, my pa laid plans to unscramble us from the clutches of his sisters-in-law. He had wanted all along to bring his family together at the same table, but he couldn't muster the courage to challenge Aunt Louise, Aunt Bridget, and Aunt Katie. The fact of the matter was that he was too dependent on them. They did, after all, give him and ma and me and Sis food for our table and a roof over our head, and that was something he was not able to do for us himself.

It was clear to the eye that my three aunts were sisters. Each had the red-rust hair of my Grandpa O'Kelly. They each had a pale, milky skin with the hint of a freckle or two. Each of them was bosomy to a fault, and that too, must have come from the O'Kelly women. Even Grandpa O'Kelly was a bit wide of chest.

My ma didn't have the O'Kelly look, except for the goat-milk skin. Her hair was as dark as a moonless tidewater night, and her breasts were the size of opened marsh oyster shells. My ma didn't share any of my aunt's arrogance either. My three aunts were very determined ladies. They bossed their husbands. They bossed their neighbors. They bossed their dogs. And they bossed my ma and my pa except when my pa could drink up enough courage to meet their eye.

So as I said, my pa could drink up some courage when he had a job that paid well enough for him to purchase his spirits. He had been working steadily as a night watchman on the wharf, and Aunt Katie got him a day job painting rooms at the Charleston Hotel. He had plenty of work and plenty to drink. So when my pa felt my ma was well enough to tend to Sis and me, he decided then to dislodge us from the clutches of his hated in-laws.

Sis and I had been attending Saint Joseph's Catholic School in Charleston. It was the same school where our cousins went. Aunt

Louise and Aunt Bridget saw to that. They would have nothing less than a good Catholic education for Sis and me. I was in the second grade, and Sis was in the fifth.

It was a Friday afternoon when my pa decided he would bring his family back together again. He had no painting to do that day, and by noon he had drunk up enough courage to face my aunts. He was at Aunt Bridget's house, where Sis and I were staying that month, when Sis and I and Aunt Bridget's two kids, cousins Ellen and Little Frankie, arrived from school. My pa and Aunt Bridget were already swapping opinions when we arrived.

"Jakey, you can't take those girls with you. Delia ain't well enough to take care of them," Aunt Bridget said, trying to remain calm while reasoning with my drunk pa.

"They are my damned girls. I'll take care of them and their ma too," my pa said, already beginning to raise his voice.

Sis and I and Ellen and Little Frankie stopped at the bottom of the stoop to listen to my pa and Aunt Bridget discuss my ma's health. They were on the first-floor porch and had not seen us yet.

"What about school?" Aunt Bridget continued her reasoning. "You can't take them out of school."

"Hell, woman, I ain't taking them to Kalamazoo. I just want my two girls to live with me in my house. They can still go to your precious damned school."

Sis, by now ahead of me and Ellen and Little Frankie, was on the first step of the side porch. She broke in, "Pa, what is it?"

As my pa turned toward Sis's voice, he almost fell from the porch. Aunt Bridget made no attempt to break his fall.

Holding onto the porch banister my pa spoke to Sis. "Sis, you and Muff get your stuff. Aw, just get some things. I will get the rest of it later. We are going to our own damned house."

"Jakey, I am not going to allow this," Aunt Bridget interrupted, and I could tell she was getting angry.

"Just how in the eternal hell are you going to stop me from getting my own damned children?" my pa yelled at Aunt Bridget, with an anger she could not approach.

Aunt Louise, who lived only two houses down from Aunt Bridget, had seen my pa when he first staggered up Guignard Street on his way to Aunt Bridget's. She had called Uncle Frank, Aunt Bridget's husband, to come home immediately. Uncle Frank was a fireman with the Charleston Fire Department, so he made it home in short order. Uncle Frank and Aunt Louise arrived at the same time. They hit the porch just as my pa was asking Aunt Bridget how she was going to stop him from getting his own damned children. My pa was outmanned by three, but Uncle Frank took command.

"Jakey Knight, what in Holy Mary's name is going on here?" Uncle Frank asked my pa, in the same patronizing voice he always used when he spoke to my pa. Uncle Frank gave off an air of being special, of being more special than he really was. He was a precinct captain with the Charleston Fire Department, a position which he equated to being mayor of Charleston. Like my aunts, Uncle Frank had no respect for my pa, but he, unlike my aunts, never even tried to hide his contempt.

"What the hell does it look like, as if you didn't already know? I am taking my damned girls to my damned home, and there ain't a damned thing you or your damned snot of a wife can do about it."

My pa had a need to pepper his language on occasion—like when he was angry or when his was drinking, and it seemed that he was one or the other most of the time. He told me that all sailors talked that way.

"Jakey Knight, you have no need to talk like that in front of the ladies and the children," Uncle Frank said to my pa, still talking to my pa as if he were a child himself.

"Now don't that beat all to hell. You [tell me how to raise my girls. You tell me want to tell me how to talk. Well, Frank, v of my tongue so you can make it say exactl

"Jakey, I think we have heard about enc said, ignoring the invitation to hold my pa home now. You are drunk and you need to so

"Well Franklin, that is exactly what I inten ⌐go home," my pa said to Uncle Frank. Then, turning to me and Sis, he said, "Come on girls. We ain't wanted in Frank and Bridget's manor."

"Jakey Knight, for the last time, the girls are staying here. You ain't fit to raise them, and Delia's too ill. Jakey, face it. You are just a stupid, crippled, drunk," Uncle Frank said to my pa, thinking that would end it all. Uncle Frank then turned to my cousins. "Frankie, Ellen, you take Nora and Mary Margaret in the house. Their father is going home now."

My pa's face turned redder than one of Uncle Frank's fire trucks. I wasn't sure if it was from his anger or from the cheap spirits. He bent over, reached under the trousers of his shriveled polio leg, and pulled out a butcher's knife that he had strapped to the brace that gave his leg strength. He touched the knife to uncle Frank's nose, and then, just as quickly, he allowed the blade to flip the bill of uncle Frank's fire captain's hat. The flipped fire captain's hat landed on one of Aunt Louise's large O'Kellian breasts and teetered there as if it might be a perfect fit for one of her seven and one-eighth tits. Slowly, the captain's hat fell to the first step leading up to aunt Bridget's veranda. Sis picked up the hat and herded me and Ellen and Little Frankie to the porch landing and out of harm's way, just in time to avoid Uncle Frank's fall.

Uncle Frank's knees had buckled, and he sat on the porch as if someone had pulled a chair from under him. Aunt Louise ran back

ouse screaming, "Jesus, Joseph, and Mary. Jakey Knight has
Frank."

Aunt Bridget stepped inside the screened door as quickly as Uncle Frank had sat down on the porch. She locked the screen door behind her and me and Sis and Little Frankie and cousin Ellen.

My pa didn't say another word. He stepped over Uncle Frank, who was still sitting on the porch, walked over to where Aunt Bridget was holing up, and very neatly cut the bottom section of the screen door. He laid the cut section of the screen door on Uncle Frank's hatless head. He reached inside the half-screened door and took Sis by the hand. "Let's go home girls," he said.

Sis took me by the hand as we stepped through the perfectly cut hole in Aunt Bridget's screen door. Sis and I helped my pa down the steps from Aunt Bridget's porch. We got on either side of him to steady his walk. After all, he was a cripple.

Chapter 2

Moving Day

Unbeknownst to Uncle Frank, Aunt Bridget, and Aunt Louise, my pa had rented an apartment on State Street for his family. So after my pa had removed us from behind the screen door at Aunt Bridget's, he immediately took Sis and me to Aunt Katie's to get my ma before Aunt Katie got home from the hotel. My pa was about choked to the gills with O'Kelly women and wanted to rid himself and his family from Aunt Katie's grip as quickly as possible.

My pa had rented a furnished upstairs apartment from Red Robertson's mother. He got it for six dollars a week. With his working two jobs he would be able to pay if he didn't stay drunk.

As I said before, my ma was a bit addle minded from her bout with the sleeping sickness, and she couldn't gather on to the fact that she was going to be living in a place of her own. It was difficult for the three of us to relay that fact to her. All her life she had lived with one relative or another.

"Delia, get your things together. We are moving. I got us a place over on State Street," my pa said, breaking the news to her.

"Oh no, oh no. Oh no," my ma said, speaking more to herself than to any of us.

Even though he was still drunk my pa tried to settle my ma with his voice. "Delia, get your things. Sis and Muff and you and me are moving." Then he said to me and Sis, "Sis, you and Muff help your ma get her clothes together. I'll get my things."

Ma began to wring her hands, as she always did when she was nervous—which was most of the time. She mumbled to none of us in particular, "I have to have Katie's supper ready at six-o'clock. I can't leave just yet."

"That old bitch-woman can cook her own supper," my pa said, losing his settling voice. "She ain't feeble." Then he went back to his settling voice, "Delia, now get your damned stuff together."

Sis took my ma by the hand. I took the other one and we urged her into the bedroom that she and my pa shared. The three of us were able to get all the clothes that my ma owned. My pa, was able to get all his clothes into one paste board box.

"What am I going to tell Katie?" my ma asked my pa as we were leaving. "She will think something has happened to us. I best leave her a note."

"Delia, don't worry about it. She will know why we are leaving. That son-of-a-bitch brother-in-law of yours is probably already down at the hotel telling her about it—if he's gotten up off the porch yet," my pa said to her, laughing at the thought of Uncle Frank still on Aunt Bridget's porch. "I'll leave her a note."

He did.

Katie, me and Delia and the girls have found us a place over on State Street with Mrs. Robertson. I am sure that Bridget and Louise will tell you all about it. Thank you for letting us stay with you. Tell Bridget that I will come by next week to pick up the rest of the girls' things. Jakey

"Now the mighty Miss Katie O'Kelley will know that the Knight leeches are gone," my pa said as he left his note of departure on Aunt Katie's lamp table, beside her favorite settee—the one where Sis was conceived.

My pa picked up his box of clothes, and the four of us set off for our new home. We looked as if we were going on a jungle movie safari. My pa blazed the way with his box on his shoulder. My ma, talking to herself while avoiding the cracks on the sidewalk, was only inches behind my pa. Sis, third in line, was ever protective of me, looking back to see that I was keeping step with the crusade of Knights. My ma's dresses, which I was toting, draped over each of my shoulders. Her funeral dress dragged to the ground, causing me to step on the hem as I struggled to keep up with my staggering pa leading his family of transients.

My pa trekked us down East Bay Street past the Market. Right at East Bay Street and Cumberland, my pa fell down trying to shift his box of clothes from one shoulder to the other. My ma, who was still counting sidewalk cracks, plowed on top of him.

"What the hell are you doing, Delia?" my pa asked from under my ma.

"Avoiding cracks. I don't want to break my ma's back."

"Damn, Delia. Your ma is dead," my pa said as he pulled himself from under my ma and back to his feet.

My ma, still on the sidewalk and covered with dresses and gowns and shoes, looked up at my pa and said, "But her back ain't broke, Jakey. She's still got a strong back."

"Damn" was all my pa could think to say.

I caught up with my family as they turned down Cumberland Street. We passed by where the "Bucket of Blood" used to be before the city closed it and by my grand-ma's old boardinghouse. My pa didn't look up to take notice. He just wanted to get his family circus off the streets of Charleston and into their new home.

Chapter 3

Skipping School

That summer at Mrs. Robertson's apartment was the happiest days of my life. My pa wasn't drinking as much since he had to use his money to pay Mrs. Robertson her six dollars a week. My ma wasn't any better, but she wasn't getting any worse either. For the first time in my life, I understood what a family was, and I loved my family, but that summer ended quickly.

When school started back after Labor Day, I was going into the third grade and Sis was going into the sixth grade. But Sis decided that we didn't need to be going back to school. With Sis and me no longer being under the wardenship of Aunt Bridget and Aunt Louise, we were free and out of control. My pa was working most of the time. He still painted at the Charleston Hotel and still did watchman duty at the wharf at night. He slept in between jobs. My ma was at home with Sis and me, but it seemed that she was more away than was our pa.

We were still enrolled at Saint Joseph's Catholic School, the same school we had attended the year previous when we were boarding with Aunt Bridget and Aunt Louise. We went for the first week of school until Sis decided that school was interfering with our education. For the next two weeks, we dressed for school, took the lunches that Ma had packed for us, and headed for school. Of course, Sis and I never arrived at Saint Joe's. Sis and I explored the streets of Charleston—that is until the day we were caught.

On that day Sis took me to the Battery. The Battery, located at the very end of Charleston, is a high sea wall designed to keep the Atlantic Ocean out of the city, and it is the place where Charleston started the war with the Yankees who had stolen Fort Sumter.

I wanted to go back to school, even though I didn't like the nuns who were my teachers. They made me do numbers on the blackboard, and when I didn't do my numbers correctly, they would hit my hands with a ruler. Sis would have no part of that, though. She disliked the nuns even more than I, and they hit her with more than just rulers. Sis would have no part in our going back to school.

"Muff," she said to me as she crawled over the wall of the Battery to step onto the slight ledge that was exposed at low tide. "I'm going to jump in the Charleston Harbor if you go back to school."

"Sis," I begged. "I won't ever go back to school. Please don't jump."

"Why shouldn't I jump? You don't love me," she said, continuing to taunt me.

I continued my pleas. "I love you. Please don't jump. Come back up. Please don't jump."

She began to shuffle along the ledge of the Battery wall, holding on to the railing as the waves egged her on to tease me even more. Sis was daring. I had seen her hang upside down over the second-floor porch railing at Aunt Bridget's until Little Frankie and cousin Ellen and I all cried.

I began to shake like the jellyfish that were waiting in the Charleston Harbor to sting Sis when she jumped into the greasy water. "If you really loved me, you would give me your lunch," she finally said.

This was something I never understood about Sis. She was protective of me around other people, and while she wouldn't let other people or the nuns at school pick on me, she herself could be cruel and unmerciful to me.

"You can have my lunch. Just don't jump in the ocean," I cried to her, the tears she had provoked washing down my face.

We had lunch at Battery Park. That is, Sis had lunch at Battery Park. She ate both our sack lunches that Ma had packed that morning—mustard-and-baloney sandwiches with lettuce and tomatoes, and an oatmeal cookie with sweet tea. Sis was not bothered at all that I was without anything to eat.

After her lunch, we walked up East Bay Street to the US Custom House. The Custom House was, to me, a castle. It was white and massive. I thought it was more beautiful than all the churches in Charleston. It was not dirty like all the other buildings. I enjoyed just looking at it, but since we had two hours until school let out, Sis had other ideas.

"Come on," Sis shouted to me, as she ran up the steps to the Custom House. I knew what she was about to do. I had seen her do it before, and it was as foolishly knee shaking as her hanging on the ocean side of the Battery wall.

The Charleston Custom House had a shelf ledge that flanked both its leeward and windward sides. My Pa liked using nautical terms when describing things, and I do as well. The ledge separated the basement from the two main floors, but I was not really sure which way the wind blew into the building. The thing is that Sis could get onto the ledge from the front porch of the Custom House. As I said, I had seen Sis climb out on the ledge before. She would shuffle her feet with her back to the building and move to the very corner of the building. When she reached the very edge, she would tease me, just as she had done at the Battery wall with her threats of jumping off the Custom House ledge.

This day she had something else in mind for me. "You go first," she ordered.

"I will not," I said to her, but with little conviction. "I am going home to Ma."

"If you go home now Ma and Pa will know that you have been cutting school, and they will put you in reform school."

"You will go to reform school too," I shot back, trying to frighten her into abandoning what I knew she would not.

"No, I won't. If you leave, I am going to go out on the ledge and jump. I mean it this time. They can't put a dead girl in reform school. You won't ever see me again—except at my funeral."

I believed Sis this time. If I didn't go first on the ledge, she would jump. I took a step and then turned around, facing the wall. I didn't want to see where I would fall. Sis was right behind me.

"Go on," she demanded, inching closer to me.

I didn't want her to touch me. I was afraid she would push me off. I kept moving. When I got to the first corner of the ledge, I stopped.

"OK, let's go back," I said to Sis, who was still inching closer to me. After much prodding, we finally we reached the rear portico of the building. I maneuvered from the ledge to the back porch of the Custom House, thinking her suicidal ordeal had come to its insufferable conclusion.

"No, we are going all the way around the building," Sis shouted, stopping me on the top tier of stairs and halting my escape.

I began to cry, but with Sis coming toward me, I negotiated my way back to the remaining wing of the ledge. The opposite side of the Custom House seemed twenty times longer than the first side and ten times higher off the ground. I looked down only once. I didn't look down again. I just kept moving and crying, believing Sis would push me off the ledge if I stopped.

It seemed like hours that we were on the ledge. Sis said to me the words I didn't want to hear: "Let me lead."

"No!" I knew that she would have to crawl over me to take the lead, and I didn't want her to touch me. I began to move faster. By the time we got near where we had started, I was exhausted. I didn't think my legs would carry me on, but I knew that if I stopped, Sis would not.

When we made the final turn at the last corner of the building, we were welcomed by Aunt Bridget and Aunt Louise. It seemed that Mr. Maroney, a Custom House employee and a friend of Uncle Frank's, had noticed us on the ledge and called our aunts. He assumed we were still living with them. With the league of conspiracy complete, my aunts had hustled up Hasell and East Bay Streets to the Custom House.

Aunt Bridget and Aunt Louise didn't say a word to us until we were settled on the front porch of the Custom House. I suppose they didn't want to frighten us, but I could not have been any more frightened. However, as soon as we stepped onto the porch, they both lit into us like baying hounds treeing a opossum.

"What do you two think you are doing?" screamed Aunt Bridget.

"Why aren't you in school?" Aunt Louise screamed in harmony with Aunt Bridget's request to know what we were doing.

Sis lied to them. "We were both sick today. Ma said we didn't have to go to school since we were sick."

"Well, if you are sick, what in tarnation are you doing on the Custom House ledge?" asked Aunt Louise.

"We had to go to Cheney's store for some bread and milk for supper," said Sis, continuing her lie.

"Jesus, Joseph, and Mary. Child, you could have been killed out there on that ledge. Now both of you come with us. We are going to see about this," Aunt Louise said, her voice rising in anger and desperation.

Sis didn't say anything as we walked the block and a half to our home on State Street. Aunt Louise and Aunt Bridget didn't stop talking.

My ma was sitting on the porch, shelling peas and talking to herself, when Sis and I and Aunt Bridget and Aunt Louise arrived. Aunt Bridget interrupted my ma's conversation. "Delia, do you know where we found these girls?"

"I didn't know they were lost," my ma deadpanned.

"They are lost, all right," said Aunt Bridget, not letting her double meaning go unnoticed.

"And you can bet your bottom dollar that we are going to do something about it," chimed in Aunt Louise.

It was Aunt Bridget's turn. "Delia, Muffin and Sis were over at the Custom House walking around the ledge. Why, if they had fallen off, they would be dead. Lucky for them, Mr. Maroney called us. Why aren't they in school, Delia?"

"Well, Bridget, I thought they were in school," my ma said just as Sis decided to join the conversation.

"I hate school," Sis said.

"I hated school too," my ma recalled. I could tell she was thinking back to when she was in school. "The nuns screamed all the time."

"Delia, why don't you let these girls live with us?" Aunt Louise asked. "Muffin could live with me and Sis could live with Bridget."

"Now, Louise, you know Jakey Knight would never stand for that. He has too much pride. Besides, he loves those babies."

"Jakey Knight has more pride than he has brains," said Aunt Bridget. "These girls are getting on in age. Something serious could happen to them, what with his drinking and all."

"What are you saying, Bridget?" my ma asked with some clarity.

"What I am saying," Aunt Bridget continued, "is that this is no way to bring up two respectable young girls. They need proper schooling, and they need to be away from that drunken husband of yours. You know he almost killed Frank, and one of these days he is going to kill one of you when he is on one of his binges."

"I know Jakey drinks, but he wouldn't harm one of these babies. He has never laid a hand on me or them," my ma lied to Aunt Bridget. Then my ma told Aunt Bridget and Aunt Louise to leave. "You all need to leave now," she said. "Jakey might be home soon, and he wouldn't be happy to see you both here." Then she added, "Don't worry about the girls. I'll get them back in school."

"That won't do. Sis and Muffin need to be raised in some decency. Delia, you are too sick to handle two girls, and Jakey Knight is too much of a drunk. Now, please let us take them with us. We can give them things that you and Jakey can't," said Aunt Louise, making a final plea to my ma.

"You can't give them the love of a ma and pa," said my ma.

"If you won't let us raise them, we will find somebody who will let us," Aunt Bridget threatened, as she turned to Aunt Louise. "Come on, Louise. Let's get out of here before Jakey gets home."

"Bridget. Louise," my ma yelled to my two aunts as they left. "Y'all come back when you can sit a spell."

Chapter 4

The Charleston Child Welfare Bureau

It was about two weeks after Aunt Louise and Aunt Bridget had caught me and Sis on the ledge of the Custom House and had asked my ma to let them raise us that we had a visitor from the Charleston County Child Welfare Bureau. We were having our supper when the welfare lady came knocking.

"Who in the hell is that? You can't even enjoy your supper without some son-of-a-bitch pestering you," said my pa ,just as he was about to take his first bite of red rice.

"I'll get it," my ma volunteered.

"Delia, sit down and eat your supper. I'll get rid of the son-of-a-bitch," my pa said to my ma as he got up from the table to answer the door.

"Who in the hell is it?" my pa demanded from the person on the other side of the door.

"Mr. Knight? Mr. Jakey Knight?" came the hidden but power-ful voice.

"Yeah. That's my name. Now, who the hell are you?" demanded my pa.

"Mr. Knight, I am Claudia Chenault from Child Welfare. May I please come in?" said the woman's voice through the door.

"We are eating supper. Can't you come back later?" my pa asked.

"No, I am afraid I can't. I really need to come in now," the woman's voice said with an air of authority.

My pa opened the door and Claudia Chenault came right in with-out being asked. She was a big lady, dwarfing my pa. She had on a pink suit with a black hat that matched her shoes. She didn't look as if she were on welfare. She immediately said to my pa, "You and your family just keep right on eating. I just need to ask a few questions."

"What the hell do you want lady?" my pa asked her.

"Mr. Knight, let me get to the point. Our bureau has received a few complaints about the neglect of your daughters, Mary Margaret and Nora, I believe. It is my job to investigate such complaints and to make a determination," Claudia Chenault said, with an official tone to her voice.

My pa became defensive. "These girls ain't neglected. You can see that they are eating a good supper, can't you? If you look up, you can see a damn roof over their heads. They got a bedroom right back there," my pa said, pointing to our bedroom. He continued, "They got a good damned ma that takes care of them, and they got a damned pa that's working two jobs to pay for their supper, and their bedroom, and that damned roof over their head, if you will just look up."

"Mr. Knight, please. I am just doing my job. This is just an investiga-tion. That is all. There is no need to get upset," said Claudia Chenault, who didn't seem to be getting upset at all.

"I ain't getting upset, but I don't see why you people have to sneak around at night to do your investigating," my pa said. "Why can't you do your investigating in the day-light like the rest of the world?" he asked her.

"Mr. Knight, I have to see what family life is like for the girls," she said, defending herself for being in our house at supper time.

"Well, take a good damned look-see," my pa invited. "We are going to finish our supper if you don't mind," he added.

"Please, go right ahead. I just have a few questions. Now I understand the girls haven't been going to school," said Claudia Chenault.

Not one of us at the table said a word.

"Well, Mr. Knight?" she asked.

"Well, what?" my pa responded.

"Are your girls going to school?"

"Oh, I didn't know you asked a damned question. I thought you were just saying that you understood that they were not going to school," my pa said, smiling at his cleverness.

"Well, I meant—" she started, but was interrupted by my pa.

"I know what the hell you meant. I have taken care of that. They will be going to school," my pa assured her.

"Mr Knight, they have missed the first two weeks of school," Claudia Chenault persisted.

"Mrs. Chenault," my Pa said, emphasizing the "she" syllable of her name, "they have been in school the past two weeks, haven't they? I told you I have taken care of that."

"What about this incident down at the Custom House?" she asked, changing the subject. "I understand that the girls were out on the ledge. Now, that is very dangerous, don't you think?"

"Hell, I reckon it is, but kids gotta have fun. I used to do the same thing when I was a boy, and I was a cripple," my pa said, half-heartedly defending Sis and me.

"Let me ask you about your wife's health," said Claudia Chenault, changing the subject again. All the while she's writing in her notebook.

"Why in the hell don't you ask her? She's sitting right there in front of you," my pa said, shaking his head in disgust.

"Mrs. Knight?" Claudia Chenault said to my ma, as if she were about to address me or Sis or some other child.

My ma looked up for the first time since Claudia Chenault had entered the room.

Claudia Chenault asked my ma, "Do you mind if I ask you about your illness?"

My ma doesn't say much at first, but once she gets started talking, she is hard to quiet.

So she started in on her illness. "I do have a touch of that diarrhea that's been going around, but I am about over it now. I still have to watch what I eat, though. I can't eat boiled peanuts. I just love me some boiled peanuts. I get them down at the Market. You know it is better to buy them late on Saturday. They will sell their leftovers pretty cheap. If you want some, I'll give you some. I can't eat them on account of that diarrhea that's been going around. Did I tell you I had that? It's going around, you know. Both the girls got it. Jakey ain't got it yet. Been real lucky, he has. Have you got it yet? I think everybody in Charleston has had a touch of it, 'cept Jakey. I bet it ruins the boiled peanut business."

"Mrs. Knight. Mrs. Knight," Claudia Chenault almost shouted, stopping my ma before she got too carried away on the peanut economy of South Carolina. "I am not talking about your diarrhea. I am talking about your—," she hesitated to glance at her black notebook, then continued— "your encephalitis lethargica."

"Oh dear. I don't have that. Only bad women get that. My eyes are as strong today as they were when I was twenty. I have them checked every two years. All of us do…." My ma began to ramble again.

"No, no, no, Mrs. Knight," Claudia Chenault interrupted again. "I am talking about your sleeping sickness."

"Oh, my," my Ma said, giggling to herself, realizing her mistake. "I had the sleeping sickness back in 21, or was it 22? I don't remember when it was, but I haven't been to sleep in over seven years. You can ask Jakey."

"How do you feel now, Mrs. Knight?" Claudia Chenault asked, sounding as if she cared.

"Well, I feel fine, except for that touch of diarrhea I'm getting over," my ma said, about to get back to the boiled peanut economy.

Claudia Chenault had to interrupt again. "No, Mrs. Knight. I mean—do you have any side effects from the enceph—I mean the sleeping sickness?"

"She talks to herself sometimes," my pa broke in. "That ain't a crime, is it? Half the people in Charleston talk to themselves sometimes or another. You'd probably go damned crazy if you didn't."

"I see," said Claudia Chenault.

"Look lady. You don't see nothing," my pa started. "Delia cooks three square meals a day. She makes sure the girls are dressed for school. She keeps a clean house. Hell, her only real vice is that she eats too many damned boiled peanuts. She does the same thing for the girls that your ma did for you and my ma would have done for me had she lived long enough."

"What about your employment, Mr. Knight?" Claudia Chenault asked, again interrupting and changing the subject at the same time.

"What about it?" my pa asked, showing his ire at being interrupted in the midst of a good argument in defense of ma.

"I mean, what do you do for a living?"

"As if you didn't already know. I am sure it is plastered in that little black book you are carrying around. I am a damned housepainter, and if you will get the hell out of my house, I can get a nap before I have to go to my other job down at the wharf," my pa said, calling an end to Claudia Chenault's visit.

"One last thing, Mr Knight," Claudia Chenault said as she made her way to our door. "It has been brought to my attention that you may have a drinking problem."

My pa was going to have the last word. He said to Claudia Chenault as he escorted her to the door, "Now I wonder who brought that to your attention? You can tell those three sisters-in-law of mine to mind their own business. Hell, each of them nips on the sherry, and Frank is as big a drunk as you will find between the Ashley and the Cooper. As a matter of fact, Delia is the only sober one in their family." My pa continued to get his feelings off his chest. "Hell, I admit I drink a bit, but I can see that that dress you are wearing is as pink as a drunk elephant. At least I don't hide it like they do. Now, Mrs. Chenault, if you will excuse me, I have to take a nap so I won't lose my job, and these girls have to get ready for bed so they won't miss school, and Delia has to do the dishes so her house will be clean when people like you come by to visit in the middle of the night."

"I think I have seen enough," Claudia Chenault said, offering her parting word. "Mr. Knight. Mrs. Knight. Girls."

After Pa slammed the door, my ma asked him if the Child Welfare Bureau were going to take Sis and me.

"I'll kill the son-of-a-bitch that tries," my pa promised, but I could tell he had his worries.

Then Sis spoke up. "Pa, don't make us go live with Aunt Bridget and Aunt Louise. We want to live here with you and Ma."

"Don't you worry," my pa said to Sis, hugging her tightly. "You won't have to live with them. I promise you that."

My pa kept his promise, sort of. We—that is my pa and ma and Sis and I—were ordered to appear before the Charleston Child Welfare Bureau for a placement hearing.

Claudia Chenault was there, this time in a red knit suit and the same black heels she had worn when she visited our apartment on State Street. With her were four men and a lady taking notes. Claudia Chenault greeted us all, and then she opened the meeting with the following letter:

We have been struggling with this family trying to raise the standards of a mother and father who have deteriorated pathetically. Unfortunately, the mother has been a victim of sleeping sickness since shortly after the birth of her second child and a deceased twin and since that time seemingly has been totally incapable of disciplining her children. She is from extremely good Irish stock, and this is apparent from meeting with her three sisters, Mrs. Frank Conlon, Mrs. G. L. McWilliams, and Miss Katie O'Kelly. These three sisters to Delia Knight have assisted untiringly to make life better for this family—in fact, they have tried to care for the children in their homes—but always the father has become resentful and made an extremely unpleasant situation. Since the age of five, he has been badly crippled but has managed to work. However, he has abused his wife and indulged inconsistently with the children, and the result is a turmoil. Upon two or three occasions, reports have come to us that the older daughter has been begging and the parents have only been belligerent in responding. The same is true of truancy to school.

We had planned for the minors' sake to take the problem before the probate court, hoping at least to obtain temporary custody. Mrs. Knight's sisters, however, dreaded so much having the children involved in court that they offered finally to persuade the Knights to sign an application for admission to the orphanage after Mrs. Conlon's offer to take the children permanently was refused. It did not seem advisable to force her offer into effect, because we knew the parents would retaliate in some way before she could do any material good. She volunteered, along with Mrs. McWilliams, to

supply all the clothing and contribute as often as possible something extra for main-
tenance. In addition, she could consider assuming the care of both children at the end
of a year's time if parents were still unfit for provision.

With the antagonism of Mr. and Mrs. Knight to any plan that will take their
children from them and the evident devotion of the children to them, which will block
any move which may strive to show the parents' incompetency, it seems at present
impossible to consider but the only thing—the orphanage—particularly since the
matter of placement should be temporary.

The sooner the case can be settled, the better for all, as the Knights are apt to
change their minds. Furthermore, the family of Mrs. Knight wishes to return to some
degree of regularity in their lives.

Claudia Chenault   11-4-1929

After reading her letter, Claudia Chenault told everyone that Mrs. Conlon, Mrs. McWilliams, and Miss O'Kelly had offered to pay five dollars each per month toward the girls upkeep. My pa said something about blood money. My pa wanted to say more, but one of Claudia Chenault's gentlemen friends told him to hold his tongue.

My pa held his tongue, but Claudia Chenault had more to say. She told the men and the lady taking notes, "I suggested to Mrs. Knight's sisters that, in the event that we accept the children, they call on the sisters at the orphanage to give them the back-ground and home-environment scenario so the sisters can better handle them. From what I have learned, the older child will require some special treatment, sympathy, and understanding guidance for some time until she gets a more reasonable attitude toward the responsibilities of a girl of eleven years."

She said that as if Sis weren't even sitting there. This stirred my pa even more. He cussed and argued some more, but Claudia Chenault paid him no mind.

"Mr. Knight, you have two choices. These girls will live with their aunts until you can better care for them, or they will be placed in the Catholic orphanage."

She then revealed to him some papers signed by a judge. Ma and Pa cussed the judge's name, but Claudia Chenault, even calmer than when she had visited our home during her investigation, told him that his bad language would not help matters. "The decision has been made," she told him with some finality.

My pa swore that he would take them to court and take his girls back, but he never did. He didn't have the money to fight them all. He kept his promise to Sis and me, though. We never had to live with Aunt Bridget and Aunt Louise.

On November 8, 1929, seven days after my eighth birthday, the Charleston Child Welfare Bureau placed Sis and me in the Sisters of Charity of Our Lady of Mercy Orphanage.

Chapter 5

Orphans

The walk from State Street to Queen Street to the Catholic orphanage was unlike our family's trek from Aunt Bridget's to our home at Mrs. Robertson's. This time we did not walk like a zig-zag circus clown parade. I was not stepping on the hem of my ma's funeral dress. She was wearing it now. There were no family pileups. My pa was as sober as the nun who greeted us at the orphanage's gate. We were a family walking hand in hand, but we would not be a family for long.

The citadel of the orphanage was more secure than Fort Sumter. A six-foot-high wall kept the Charlestonians out and the orphans in. Sis and I were to be separated from all of Charleston, including my ma and pa.

Sis and I had visited the orphanage wall before. In fact, she had tried to climb it so that she could threaten to jump off in an attempt to separate me from my brown-bag school lunch, but the orphanage wall was one piece of stonework in Charleston that she was not able to conquer. The ominous warning was that she would not be able to escape from the inside either.

We had always known about the orphans on the inside. We could always hear the little ones whenever Sis was trying to scale the orphanage wall. Our pa would even joke about putting us in there whenever we pestered him, but we had never fathomed that we would join the exiled waifs on the inside, and neither had our pa.

The sober nun was not the only greeter at the Sisters of Charity of Our Lady of Mercy Orphanage. Of course, Aunt Louise, Aunt Bridget, and Aunt Katie were there. My Pa was too full of tears to cuss them. He had been crying since we left our home and was not able to work up a *hell*, or *damn* or *son-of-a-bitch* to throw at my aunts. Strangely, my ma had not cried at all. She simply wrung her hands—her way of crying without letting tears get in the way.

At the sight of the orphanage's gate Sis and I joined in with our pa to produce a nice chorus of tears with sobs. We took our tears in with us, but Aunt Bridget stopped us abruptly on the top step of the admissions building.

"You girls can stop that crying right now," she demanded. Then she said, with her best attempt at compassion, "There is nothing to be afraid of. They will take good care of you here. Just remember, this is the best thing for you."

Sis and I were not convinced by our aunt's assurance. Our doubt followed us, as the sober nun, who had not said a word since she greeted us at the orphanage gate, escorted us into the double-wide entrance to our new home.

The orphanage had many names. Ma simply called it the orphanage. My aunts, very formally, identified it as the Charleston Catholic Asylum to distinguish it from the city orphanage on Calhoun Street or the Jenkins Orphanage for colored children. My pa, at least until we were incarcerated there, referred to it as the Queen Street House for Guttersnipe.

The building had a history dating back to before the Civil War. It had served as the mother house for the Sisters of Charity of Our Lady of Mercy but soon became a home for Catholic orphans. It survived the Civil War, barely. The residents had to abandon the building when a Union bomb struck nearby. Over the years, it took a beating from the Charleston weather. It was mauled by the overpowering summer heat and scarred by the random Atlantic storms. Yet it stood strong, even through recent neglect from lack of funds and changing economic tides.

Entering the orphan house itself, we were met with a familiar odor—old school-house mildew with a tinge of boiling cabbage creeping along the walls. There was a long row of foreboding stairs facing us as we entered. My immediate thought was that I did not want to scale those stairs. Though not as lofty as the steps to the Charleston Custom House, the stairs to the second floor of this Provost Dungeon left me with the same fear of expectation as when Sis would take me to the ledge of the Custom House and threaten to jump.

I was as uneasy as a crab being made ready for a boil and my stomach was as knotted as a ball of my Ma's knitting yarn. Sis, on the other hand, was ready for a fight. She showed no fear. She was as snarly as a King Street cur about to be muzzled by the city dogcatcher, determined not to be necklaced by the nuns.

The nun who greeted us at the gate disappeared just as quickly as a second nun approached us. I could tell from her entrance into the foyer that she was the Mother Superior. She immediately took control.

"Good day, everyone," she opened. "I am Sister Beatrice. I have been expecting you. And how are you, Delia?" She turned to my ma. "It is very nice to see you, even under these dire circumstances. Could I have a word with you, please?"

Sister Beatrice knew my ma from the cathedral where my ma attended mass. I could not hear their private conversation, but my ma stopped wringing her hands for the time they were talking.

When Sister Beatrice and my ma finished their private conversation, the good sister turned to my three aunts and said with a curtness that offended each of them, "You ladies may leave now. I think Delia and Mr. Knight can handle things from here on. We won't be needing you."

As my aunts turned in a huff and left the foyer. Sister Beatrice turned to Sis and me with an introduction: "Nora. Mary Margaret. I am Sister Beatrice, and I want to welcome you both." Sister Beatrice reached to shake our hands. My grip was as limp as an East Bay Street wino's. Sis's hand-shake, on the other hand, was as strong as the incoming tide. Sister Beatrice, standing like the Battery wall, paid Sis no never mind.

Next, she turned to my ma and pa, but addressed my ma because my pa was still crying without control. "Delia, I think it best that you and Mr. Knight not stay around. It will be easier on the girls."

Sister Beatrice then turned back to Sis and me, and without much compassion, said, "Nora, you and Mary Margaret say your good-byes to your mother and father"

I wrapped my arms around my ma's bony legs and buried my face in her black funeral dress.

Ma grabbed Sis by the shoulders, kissed her cheek, and whispered, "Give them as much trouble as you can so they will let you out of here."

Sister Beatrice tried to pry me loose from my ma's leg, but I wouldn't release until Sis touched my shoulder and said to me, "Come on Muff. Ma has to go back home now."

Sister Beatrice took Sis by the hand, and Sis took me by the hand as the three of us moved toward the stairs, and so began our orientation to our new home. "The girls' quarters are on the right wing of the building. The boys' are on the left. Under no circumstances are you to go into the boys' quarters, and you must report any boy who enters your area. The younger girls are housed on the second floor, with Sister Barbara. Mary Margaret, you will meet Sister Barbara momentarily. Nora, you will be with the older girls on the main floor, with Sister Teresa. The dining hall is in the basement. After Sister Barbara and Sister Teresa get you acquainted with your rooms, they will give you your work assignments. All the boys and girls must pull their loads. Now, do you have any questions?"

I, of course, had no questions. My fear would not have allowed me to speak even if I did have a question. Sis had no such fear. "Yes, Sister. I do have a question," Sis ventured. "When are we getting out of this dump?"

Sister Beatrice's eyebrows disappeared under the white band of her hooded head. She almost screamed at Sis, "Young lady, let me assure you that that tone and sass will not be tolerated here." Calming a bit, she added, "Now both of you wait here while I get Sister Barbara and Sister Teresa."

Sister Teresa appeared first. Short and wide, Sister Teresa had the look of many of my male O'Kelly relatives. "Sister Teresa, these are Mary Margaret and Nora Knight," introduced Sister Beatrice. "Watch this one," she said, eyeing Sis. "She has a mouth on her."

"We will see about that," said Sister Teresa as she pried my hand free from my sister's with one single jerk and led Sis off to the big girls' quarters on the first floor. As Sister Teresa turned with Sis, she crashed into Sister Barbara.

Sister Barbara was the size of my ma, but she was prettier than my ma. Sister Barbara had the look of a movie star who was playing a nun. Years later, when I saw Ingrid Bergman in *The Bells of St. Mary's* with Bing Crosby, images of Sister Barbara emerged from my days at the orphanage.

As soon as she recovered from being bulldogged by Sister Teresa, she said, even before Sister Beatrice could introduce us, "I'll bet this is Mary Margaret. Do they call you Mary or Margaret or both?"

"My ma and pa and Sis call me Muff," I said, relaxing under the spell of her smiling beauty. "Everybody else calls me Mary Margaret."

"Then I will call you Mary Margaret like everyone else. We will let "Muff" be special for your mother and father and sister. I am Sister Barbara. I am in charge of the younger girls on the second floor. You will be living up stairs with me," she said, as she took me by the hand and led me up the stairs to my dormitory.

"How old are you, Mary Margaret?" Sister Barbara asked when we reached the top of the stairs.

"I am eight years old. I had my birthday last week," I answered, in a voice that was stronger than the one I had left at the bottom of the stairs.

"My, you are a little one, aren't you?"

Before I could answer her question about my size, she placed her hand on my shoulder and pulled me closer to her.

"Come, I will show you where you will be sleeping."

Supper was at five o'clock sharp. Sister Barbara had to wake me up. The other girls on my floor had already lined up and were waiting for Sister Barbara to take us down to the dining hall. She waited for me to use the toilet and then let me hold her hand as we walked down the two flights of stairs to the basement dining hall.

Sis's group had already seated themselves. I spotted Sis immediately. She was seated with the other big girls across the dining hall from where Sister Barbara had seated us.

"Sister Barbara, can I eat with Sis?" I asked.

"Well, you have to eat with your age group, but I think you can eat with your sister today," she said as if she had anticipated my request.

Sister Barbara took me by the hand and led me to Sis's table. There was an empty chair next to Sis. In fact, no one was sitting near her. Sister Barbara left me alone to be with Sis.

"Hey, Sis," I said, smiling at her.

"What are you smiling at?"

"Sister Barbara said I could sit with you during supper," I said without answering her question about my smile. "I can't do it anymore after today, though. I have to eat with my group from now on."

Sister Teresa, who was sitting at the head of one of the big girls' tables, stood up about the time I finished explaining to Sis the eating arrangements. All the big girls stood up with her and in single file marched to the serving line.

"Why are you sitting at this table?" Sister Teresa asked me as she passed Sis and me on her way to the serving line.

"Sister Barbara said I could sit with Sis," I said, barely audible but still smiling at my good fortune at being able to sit with Sis.

"Well, as long as it is just for tonight's supper. The two of you need to get in line with the rest of the girls. Just follow them."

There were a number of bigger boys and girls working in the kitchen and on the serving line. Just as Sis was telling me that Sister Teresa had told her that she would be working in the kitchen, Sister Teresa walked up behind us and said that there would be no talking in the serving line.

"I was telling Muff that you might let me work in the kitchen," Sis said to her, giving an explanation for our conversation.

"I don't care if you were telling Pope Pius himself. I said no talking in the serving line."

"Yes, ma'am," Sis answered, as if she were responding to a Parris Island drill sergeant.

"Yes, ma'am," I said politely, as if I were talking to Sister Teresa.

Sis and I didn't say another word until we had gotten our food trays filled and sat down at Sis's assigned table. Sister Teresa sat down across from us. We felt uncomfortable with her being across from us, so we only talked about our rooms.

We had better food to eat at home. For our first orphan's supper, we had green peas, beets, rice and gravy, and a slice of canned peach. We had water to drink. I ate the peach first, and that didn't sit well with Sister Teresa. She told me to save my dessert for last. She also interrupted Sis's meal when she told her not to drink her water until she had finished everything else on her plate.

Sis and I were very cautious about the order in which we ate our food. I ate the food I liked best first, which was the rice and gravy. Then I ate my peas. My plate was clean, except for the beets.

"Mary Margaret, eat your beets," Sister Teresa demanded as Sis and I started to get up from the table to put our trays away as the other girls were doing.

"She don't like beets," Sis said, beginning to start an explanation of my dietary habits.

"I don't care if she likes them or not. We are not going to waste food here. If you put food on your plate, the rule is that you must eat every bit of it. No waste."

"She didn't put beets on her plate. They stuck beets on her plate," Sis argued in my defense.

I was beginning to think that I should have eaten supper with Sister Barbara and the other little girls when Sister Teresa interrupted my thoughts with a growl and a scowl. "Miss Nora, no one is talking to you. Therefore, keep your mouth to yourself, or it is going to get you in serious trouble."

Sister Teresa then turned to me, and by this time I had begun to well up with tears. "Mary Margaret, you are not going to leave this table until you eat all your beets. You might as well dry up those tears. We will stay here until the Second Coming if need be."

"Here, Muff, I will eat them for you," Sis said as she grabbed a handful of beets off my plate and stuffed them into her mouth.

This infuriated Sister Teresa, and as Sis reached for her second handful, helping to finish off my beets, Sister Teresa slapped at her hand with her fork. The fork scraped across the top of Sis's hand. I couldn't tell beet juice from blood, but it looked as if Sis was bleeding from both her hand and her mouth. Sis dropped her second helping of my beets as Sister Teresa was preparing a second swipe at her bleeding, beet red hand.

Then Sister Teresa screamed at the two of us, "Nora Knight, you just earned yourself punishment time. Take yourself out of here, and I will be up to deal with you later. And you, Mary Margaret, eat those beets. Now!"

Conversation in the dining hall ceased as everyone focused on Sister Teresa, Sis, and me. Sister Barbara came over to see what was the matter and asked that very question of Sister Teresa.

"The matter is that little Miss Mary Margaret doesn't seem to want to eat all her food," Sister Teresa said in a voice much nicer than the one she had employed with Sis and me but still laced with a bit of anger.

Sister Barbara patted my head and then cupped my cheeks in both her hands. "I'm sorry dear, but you have to eat everything on your plate. That is the rule. But next time don't get any of those old nasty beets."

I knew that the beets would not square with me. That night, after lights out, I began to get stomach cramps. I lay quietly, thinking of my ma and pa, trying to forget about the pain in my belly. It would not go away. Getting out of bed, I saw that all the other girls on my floor were asleep. I remembered where the toilet was from when I had gone after my afternoon nap before suppertime and from the after-supper washup. There wasn't much light in the room, but it was easy to make my way between the two rows of beds that lined either side of the long room.

Just as I got to the toilet, which was a side room at the far end of our sleep room, I heard a voice I easily recognized as Sister Teresa's. "Where to, please?"

"Oh! Sister Teresa," I said, with an obvious startle. "I have to go to the toilet. I think I am going to vomit. My stomach hurts."

"Don't give me that, young lady. Didn't you go to the ladies' room after supper?"

"Yes Sister, but I'm—."

She didn't let me finish. "Then march yourself right back out there and get in your bed," she demanded. "You have another thing coming if you think I am going fall for that story. Those beets didn't make you sick. Beets, indeed."

Tears flushed my eyes as I made my way back to my bed. I momentarily forgot the pain in my stomach. That is, until I threw up beets, peaches, peas, and rice and gravy all over my pillow. I removed the pillow from its case, being careful not to spill any of the vomit on my sheets. I placed the pillowcase on the floor beside my bed. The vomit had soaked through to my pillow. I placed the pillow on the floor beside the soaked case. That night, my first night in the orphanage, I cried with no pillow to cry on.

Chapter 6

The Rebel and the Evil Nuns

Sis's punishment time for eating my beets was for one month. She was confined to her room, denied any privileges, and given extra work detail. And of course, it meant that she lost visitation rights when my ma and pa came to see us in December. This made Pa mad, and he let them know it too, but he still didn't get to see Sis.

While my pa was yelling at Sister Beatrice, my ma told Sister Barbara that my pa had lost his job as a night watchman down at the wharf and that he wasn't painting as much as he had been prior to our being placed in the orphanage. My ma figured that my trio of evil aunts had a hand in my pa's loss of employment. As long as he was struggling, we were assured a long stay in the orphanage. I heard my ma tell Sister Barbara that they might be moving from State Street because they could no longer afford to pay Mrs. Robertson her six dollars each week.

As things turned out, my ma was right. When it was time for their January visit my ma and pa didn't show up. Uncle Frank came by on the January visitation Sunday and took us to his house for visitation. In fact, for the next six months, Sis and I didn't get to see our ma and pa. Uncle Frank told us that they had moved to Sullivan's Island.

Sullivan's Island is one of those long, skinny islands that protect South Carolina from the Atlantic Ocean. There wasn't much there at that time. Old Fort Moultrie was on one end of the island and there was a sprinkling of white beach houses that dotted the middle of the island.

The island used to be a hangout for pirates, and it was made famous when some guy, I can't remember his name, wrote about pirates looking for a gold bug. Aunt Bridget, Aunt Louise, and Aunt Katie each owned a house on Sullivan's Island. They rented them to rich Yankees during the summer and poor Charlestonians during the winter.

Pa later explained their move this way:

"When I lost my damned job at the wharf, I couldn't afford to pay Mrs. Robertson her rent money. I offered to work on the house for room. God knows the house needed work. Hell, I told her I would paint the whole damned thing for six months' rent, but she told me she couldn't eat a paint job. She needed the money, what with the Depression and all. On top of all that, I wasn't getting much work at the hotel either.

"Your ma and I were about to be put out on the street till Frank offered us his place on the island. I guess his damned conscience was getting the best of him. He allowed that me and your ma could stay there rent—free if I painted the damned place and kept it up. He said we could stay there until I got back on my feet. Now ain't that a hell of a thing to say to a damned cripple. When does he think I will ever get back on my feet?

"Well anyway," Pa continued. "I got some work at Fort Moultrie. Some of the barracks were in need of a paint job, and your ma raises chickens. She sells the eggs, and we eat some of the chickens. She has already planted some early vegetables. We have been eating greens and cabbage."

My pa offered this apology. "We can't see you and Sis like we hoped we could. It costs a quarter every time we cross the Cooper River to come into Charleston. We don't have that extra every month. That is the reason we haven't been to visit you this year. We just haven't had the damned money, but things are bound to get better."

But things never did get better. Just about every month, on visitation Sunday, we would go over to Aunt Bridget's or Aunt Louise's. Sometime our ma would come by our aunt's house to visit, but my pa would never do that. He refused to step a foot in their house. On rare occasions, when the chickens were laying a lot of eggs and my ma and pa had a spare quarter, they would visit us at the orphanage.

So that was it. Sunday after Sunday we waited to see if my ma and pa would be able to visit. More often than not, we ended up at one of our aunts' homes. We didn't like the arrangement, but it was a chance to breathe some fresh air.

As the months passed, Sis seemed to get angrier with age. She got into more and more trouble with the nuns and more often than not the trouble began with Sister Teresa. Her bouts with Sister Teresa meant that Sis often missed out on visitations to Aunt Louise's and Aunt Bridget's. Sometimes she even missed the rare visits from my ma and pa when they could afford the quarter to cross the Cooper River.

On Sis's sixteenth birthday our cousin Ellen gave her some old movie star magazines—magazines where you found out about the real Leslie Howard, or who Joan Bennett was dating, or if romance would wreck Joan Crawford's career. Sis loved collecting all the movie magazines of the day. She even had a scrapbook of movie star pictures, but of course she wasn't allowed to have it in the orphanage.

Sis only had the magazines that cousin Ellen had given her for a week when they turned up missing. She hadn't even had time to scissor out the pictures of Clark Gable for her scrapbook. Letting her anger get the best of her, she told Sister Teresa that someone had stolen her magazines. Sister Teresa didn't care and told Sis that it was a sin to have such trash and that God took the magazines away from her.

Sister Teresa discovered that God had not taken the magazines. In fact, it was May Beth Fogerty who had taken the magazines. God had nothing to do with it. Sister Teresa found the magazines stuffed in May Beth Fogerty's pillow-case. May Beth Fogerty said she was just looking at the magazines and was going to give them back as soon as she had finished reading about William Powell and Carole Lombard's divorce. Sister Teresa took the magazines, but didn't give May Beth Fogerty punishment time for stealing.

"If it had been me, you would have given me punishment time," Sis said to Sister Teresa with a little tone in her voice.

"Well, for being such a smart-mouth about it, I am going to give you a day on the punishment bench anyway," Sister Teresa said back to Sis, determined as ever to win the constant battle of wills.

The punishment bench was located on the main-floor foyer where we had first met Sisters Beatrice, Teresa, and Barbara—close to Sister Beatrice's office. If a girl was assigned to the punishment bench, she had to sit there all day. The sitting part wasn't so bad, even though the bench had no padding. The bad part was when the other girls would come by and make fun of you. That would hurt your feelings or make you mad.

May Beth Fogerty made the mistake of making fun of Sis while she was assigned to the punishment bench. May Beth didn't hurt Sis's feelings. I never saw anyone in the orphanage hurt Sis's feelings, but May Beth Fogerty unfurled a rage in Sis that was hard to corner once it got loose. Sis swarmed into May Beth Fogerty like a nest of stepped-on yellow jackets. By the time Sister Teresa got to them, Sis had already stuffed May Beth Fogerty under the punishment bench and was pulling her contorted hair through the slats. It took Sister Teresa, Sister Barbara, and Sister Beatrice, all three, to pry May Beth Fogerty's volcanic red hair from the grips of Sis's talons.

"We are going to have you placed in reform school!" Sister Teresa yelled at Sis.

"You can't put me anywhere. My pa and my ma are still alive, and they are paying for me to be in this nuthouse," Sis yelled back, knowing good and well that my ma and pa couldn't afford the quarter to cross the Cooper River on Sunday visitation, much less pay for our room and board.

Thanks to Sister Barbara, Sis didn't end up in reform school. She only received one month's punishment for beating up May Beth Fogerty. Sister Barbara explained to Sister Beatrice about the movie magazines and how it was May Beth Fogerty's fault in the first place for stealing Sis's magazines. May Beth Fogerty got no punishment outside of Sis giving her a double shiner, a ballooned lower lip, a bloody nose, and a licking she would have to carry with her until doomsday.

The next time my pa could afford a visit to the orphanage I told him about Sis beating up May Beth Fogerty and how Sister Teresa was always picking on Sis. He told me not to worry and that he was going to get us out of the orphanage soon. Of course, he had been saying that for five years, but somehow I got the feeling he meant it that time.

Play time at the orphanage was about as dull and routine as everything else there. There was one kickball to be shared with all the girls, but the bigger girls dominated the kickball. They turned the game of kickball into a game of "let's see who can remove a sister's veil". The object was to kick or throw the ball into the head of a playtime supervising nun.

In particular, Sister Lucy was the primary target for "let's see who can remove a Sister's veil". Sister Lucy was an evil sister. Sister Teresa was a saint compared to Sister Lucy. Sister Lucy loved boys and hated girls, and she daily made it her mission to make a girl, any girl, miserable. Sister Lucy coached the boys' basketball team and was first base coach on the boys' baseball team.

As much as Sister Lucy loved boys, she would drop a girl for the slightest of infractions. Her method of punishment was habitually a Bo-Lo paddle, sans the ball, which she secreted somewhere under her habit. She was as quick on the draw with that paddle as John Wesley Hardin was with a six-shooter, and she was twice as evil. John Wesley, however, had better aim. Sister Lucy's target of choice was invariably the head, and she had no hesitation when the blows were facial. Many an orphan girl's features were saucy red from Sister Lucy's Bo-Lo paddle.

May Beth Fogerty had yet to recover from my Sis's beating when she had the misfortune of winning the game of "let's see who can remove a Sister's veil." May Beth's ill-placed kick whacked Sister Lucy just as she was demonstrating to one of her boys the fine art of the double play. Just as I heard her say, "Stinkers forever to chance," May Beth's kicked ball hit Sister Lucy in the behind with enough force to dislodge her veil. Sister Lucy had her Bo-Lo paddle at the ready even before the laughter infested the play ground.

May Beth was frozen halfway between home base and first when the Bo-Lo paddle caught her broadside of her previously bruised head. Sis was covering first base when she realized that May Beth Fogerty was not going to be able to beat out her infield hit. May Beth Fogerty was down on her knees, praying for divine intervention as Sister Lucy continued to imprint her head with the Bo-Lo trademark. I could tell Sis was in a ticklish pickle. She could chase the errant kickball and ignore Sister Lucy as she flailed May Beth Fogerty. Or she could enjoy the beating being administered to May Beth Fogerty. Or she could separate the hated Sister Lucy from her beloved Bo-Lo.

Sis chose to take her orphaned frustrations out on the evil sister. Just as Sister Lucy was about to administer her next whack on May Beth

Fogerty's unprotected head, Sis grabbed the sister's Bo-Lo paddle with one quick swipe of her left hand and at the same time punched Sister Lucy smack in the mouth with her right. Blood shot all the way to first base. Sis didn't stop there. Her salvo continued even while Sister Lucy lay prostrate on the ground. It took the shortstop and the center fielder to dislodge Sis from her attack. Sister Lucy didn't move, and Sis went back to playing first base.

McAllister's sent over a Black Mariah to take Sister Lucy to Roper Hospital. A chorus of the bigger orphan girls gathered at home plate. As they loaded Sister Lucy into the back of the McAllister wagon, the girls sang, "Bang bang Lucy, Lucy's going away. Who is going to bang us now that Lucy is going away?"

Sis got another month of punishment and we never saw Sister Lucy again. Rumor had it that she had been cloistered up in Boston. Aside from her beating, May Beth Fogerty got to ride with Sister Lucy to Roper.

My habit during playtime was to take advantage of the swing set. Since Sis was more often than not in punishment, I was free to be alone on the play ground, and my play of choice was to swing and think of my ma and pa. I discovered that if I swung high enough I could see over the wall separating me from Charleston.

I imagined that if I swung high enough and let go of the swing's chain, I could sail over the wall into the arms of my ma and pa.

"Ma," I would cry on the first upward swing where I could see over the wall.

I would cry silently until the next swing took me to a height where I could see over the wall again. "Pa."

"Catch me," I would cry on the next swing. "I want to go home."

Then I would repeat at the height of each pendular swing, "Ma, Pa, catch me. I want to go home."

Again and again I would cry this—this prayer.

Not many days after the Sister Lucy's beating and when Sis was in punishment, I was swinging alone and crying my prayers to go home.

"Mary Margaret, why are you crying? What are you saying?"

I recognized the voice coming from behind me, but I had to slow my swing before I could talk to Sister Barbara.

"Mary Margaret, what is the matter?" asked Sister Barbara, who had by this time seated herself in the swing next to the one I was in.

"Come here," she called, in the same sweet, kind, gentle, loving voice that only she of all the sisters had used in the five years I had been imprisoned in the Queen Street fortress.

I got out of my swing and went to Sister Barbara. She immediately put her arms around me. "Mary Margaret, tell me what is wrong," she said.

An earthquake of emotion overcame me. For five years I had held it all in, too afraid to let it erupt. In the arms of Sister Barbara, I shook and wept with no control. Only the strength of her arms kept me from collapsing to the furrowed ground beneath the swing.

Finally, she said, "Here, sit in my lap. Let's swing together."

Even though I was thirteen years old at the time, at that moment in the lap of Sister Barbara, I was a child—a small child physically, and a smaller child emotionally.

Once my quaking spasms soothed into deep gasps and breathless ejaculations, Sister Barbara said to me, "I am not supposed to be telling you this, but you may be getting your wish. I understand that your father has a man who is working to get you and Nora released. Now don't get your hopes up too high because it may take a while before anything can be done. And don't tell a soul I told you this. Don't even tell Nora. This will be our own little secret. Promise?"

I held on to Sister Barbara tightly even as I gave her my promise not to tell our secret. I felt I could see over the wall even though we were hardly swinging.

Truth being stranger than fiction, my pa had indeed been talking with a lawyer about getting us out of the orphanage. Of course, my pa couldn't afford to hire a lawyer. He had been hired by Mr. Thadd Poole to paint Mr. Poole's home on James Island. While working there, he got to explaining to Mr. Poole about Sis and me being stolen by the Charleston Child Services, and about my ma's sisters, and about Mrs. Claudia Chenault. Mr. Poole agreed to help my pa get us back in exchange for a paint job.

Even further stranger than fiction—my pa really didn't need a lawyer's help after all. Sis sort of managed to bring about our release all by herself.

As I said before, it had become common practice for us to go to Aunt Bridget's or Aunt Louise's for Sunday visitation, and now that we were older, our aunts would allow Sis and me and Cousin Ellen and Little Frankie to walk to the Battery after we had Sunday lunch as long as we were back in time to return to the orphanage by our six o'clock curfew time. We looked forward to this time since it was the only time we were not under the dictates of nuns or aunts.

Sis was seventeen years old, and she had developed a keen interest in boys which she never got to prosecute while under the vigilant eye of aunts and nuns. So we were down at the Battery with cousin Ellen and Little Frankie when Sis got to talking to some young sailors who were stationed at the Charleston Navy Yard and happened to take their Sunday leave at Battery Park. There were three of them, and they all seemed a little sponged to me. I should know. My pa often had the same smell and demeanor when he was drinking.

The three sailors seemed to like Sis and cousin Ellen, especially since Ellen was bursting with an O'Kellian bust. But I was too little for them to pay me any mind. They did talk to me, though.

Sis told the three sailors that she was a college student at the Queen Street College. I could tell she was getting carried away with herself when she invited them to come to the campus to visit her anytime.

"Admiral, you should come by the campus for a visit," Sis said to the sailor Nicholson, teasing him with a flirty ranking term of endearment.

"You look too young to be in college," Admiral Phillip Nicholson said to Sis.

"You look too young to be in the navy." said Sis.

"I lied about my age, but they let me in anyway," said Admiral Nicholson.

"Yeah, I lied about my grades, but they let me in anyway."

"Where do you stay?" inquired Admiral Nicholson.

"I live in the women's dorm—Pope Pius Hall. You ever heard of it?"

"No, but I will find it," the admiral assured her.

Sis was just having a good time. It was just a little innocent flirting, but the slosh-buckling sailor thought he had fallen in love. On his next free Sunday, the swabbie took Sis at her word when he came to visit Sis at the Queen Street College.

Admiral Nicholson again had to drink up the courage to meet Sis. By the time he arrived at the Queen Street College, he was barely sober enough to scale its wall.

I didn't see what happened, but Sis told me all about it later. Admiral Nicholson, after scaling the wall, came to the girls' wing of the orphanage and began to call Sis's name as he stood outside the window at the east end of the building. Ruby Nance heard him first and ran to tell Sis that a man in uniform was outside the window calling her name.

Sis said she raced to the window and flung it open. With a handful of giggles, she whispered down to the staggering sailor, "Who goes there?"

"It is I, Admiral Phillip C. Nicholson, US Navy. Is Nora Knight aboard?"

"This is Nora," Sis whispered again. "What are you doing here? And you are no admiral."

"You invited me, and I got a promotion. Give me a hand, and I will come on board"

Sis, still engulfed in giggles and by this time joined by a hive of other gigglers from the first floor who had joined her in sparking the sottish sailor, whispered loudly to the admiral, "You can't come up here. I'll get in trouble."

"Not to worry," assured Admiral Nicholson. "I've cleared it with the dean. He gave me a visitor's pass."

As soon as Sis had opened the window, May Beth Fogerty had dashed off to retrieve Sister Teresa. May Beth had never thanked Sis for staving off the Bo-Lo Paddle from her head, and I guess she was still resentful that Sis had beaten her senseless under the punishment bench.

Sister Teresa arrived at the window just as the admiral was proclaiming that he had a visitors pass from the dean of the college. "Who is out there?" Sister Teresa asked of the gaggle of gigglers in her usual demanding voice.

None of the girls answered. They were still in giggles, gawking at the uniformed drunk who was by now trying to make his way up the shaky crepe myrtle that stood outside the girls' first-floor window.

Just as Sister Teresa stuck her veiled head out the window to get a better look, in popped the head of Admiral Phillip C. Nicholson.

"Good evening ma'am. I am Rear Admiral Phillip C. Nicholson, US Navy, reporting for duty. May I come aboard?"

"Jesus, Joseph and Mary! It's a man," shouted Sister Teresa as she began to pound on the knuckles of the sailor who was, by now, hanging from the windowsill by his finger tips.

"Someone call the police," she yelled.

Ever the volunteer, May Beth Fogerty sprinted to Sister Beatrice's office, where the only phone in the building was located, to tell Sister Beatrice to call the police because a ship load of sailors was breaking into the orphanage to elope with Nora Knight.

Sister Beatrice called the Charleston police, but instead of coming themselves, they sent the shore patrol. The shore patrol found Admiral

Nicholson passed out, lodged in a forked branch of the crepe myrtle. When they took him away, Sis said he was singing, "Nora, Nora, give me your answer, do. I'm half crazy all for the love of you."

Sister Teresa was fit to be tied. She threw Sis down on the nearest bed and started beating her with a hairbrush. That didn't last for very long. Sis had taken the hair-brush from Sister Teresa and was just beginning to give Sister Teresa what for when Sister Barbara girdled Sis in her arms, sat on the bed, and held Sis in her lap just as she had held me in the swings but with a tad more force.

Sis explained to Sister Barbara and later to Sister Beatrice about meeting the sailor at Battery Park but that it wasn't her fault that he got drunk and decided to visit her at the orphanage. Sis left out the part about her being a college student, so Sister Beatrice was satisfied and put off any punishment until she could investigate.

A sober Mr. Nicholson came by the orphanage on Wednesday to apologize for his behavior. He accepted all the blame for the incident and told Sister Beatrice that Sis should not be punished for his unforgivable behavior. The vase of flowers and the fact that Mr. Nicholson was a good Catholic boy from Polo, Illinois, put Sister Beatrice in a forgiving mood.

There was no punishment for Sis, but I think the nuns had had enough of Nora Knight. Sister Beatrice offered to Aunt Bridget, Aunt Louise, and Aunt Katie that since Sis was seventeen years old, almost an adult, she was old enough to take care of herself. She made the same suggestion to the Child Welfare Bureau. And since my pa had use of a lawyer to look into our getting released, the decision was made to return Sis to my ma and pa, and since Sis was getting her freedom, they decided to release me too. So we were released to my ma and pa on the ninth day of June, 1935.

SULLIVAN'S ISLAND, SOUTH CAROLINA 1935-1938

Chapter 7

Home Is Where the Hurt Is

Sis and I spent just over five and a half years in that misgoverned institution on Queen Street at the behest of our aunts and the City of Charleston. Even though I was surrounded by scores of children and a squadron of nuns, I was lonely for most all of those five years. Where Sis thrived on the neglect, I broke. While she never cried, I cried nightly.

And then there was the abuse. While I rarely was punished because I was too afraid to act out, Sis was, with unfailing regularity, punished for her rebellion.

Every return from Mass resulted in some form of punishment for Sis. For Sis Mass was a time when the nuns could not verbally lash out at her, so she felt no restraints to her behavior. Reverence was foreign to Sis. Her conversation during service was loud and profane.

Her "Our Father" became "Our father, who farts in heaven, hell below be thy name. Thy kingdom's dumb, thy will chew gum on earth and in heaven. Give us some hay for our daily bed, and forgive us of our tres-pisses and forgive those who tres-piss against us. Lead us not into menstruation, and deliver us from measles. For crime is the kingdom, and the flower, and the gory, for ever and never. A women." For this prayer, she spent many a Sunday afternoon in the orphan's attic, or what the nuns called isolation.

I must admit that Sis brought a lot of the suffering on herself, but for the nuns she was the lamb to be sacrificed to keep the other children of Lucifer at bay. A nun would approach Sis, trying to send a message of cleanliness and godliness to all the girls, and say, "Miss Nora Knight, your hair is a mess. All our girls are expected to look like ladies at all times. Why is your hair not groomed?"

"The brush you beat me with doesn't have any more bristles," Sis would say. "I guess you need to get us a new brush so I can have stylish hair and you can have a new head knocker."

If she refused to do her schoolwork, Sis was whacked across the hands with a ruler. When she sassed a nun, she was slammed against the wall. A raise of the eyebrow was worth an hour on the punishment bench. I don't want to give Sis any passes. As I said, she brought much of it on herself. She was defiant—a real rebel— but the viciousness of her punishment was right out of the Inquisition. I have no doubt that if the nuns had had access to an iron maiden, a rack, or witch's bridal, they would have used them to bring all the heathen orphans to the loving arms of God.

Even today I still ask myself, "Why do these people of God rage so against children? Is it the religion that is disturbed, or is it the people it attracts?"

At the very least, a rules infractions resulted in an ear pulling. A wet bed meant a day on the punishment bench with the pee-soaked bed linen draped about one's head and shoulders for all to see.

While I made a point to avoid all encounters of confrontation, there were those like Sis who cherished the crusade. The best line of defense Sis could offer was her tongue. She used it as an instrument of sass more often than not, but she would also use it as one might today use one's middle finger.

The nuns used the closet to quarantine against bad behavior. We were tormented with pinches, yardsticks, and rulers. Yelling was the orthodox language of the nun. Hair pulling was the standard mode of conveyance to draw kids in line. Chewing gum was a sin: thou shalt not chew gum. The punishment—place the gum in your hair. The cure for poor penmanship—knuckle rapping with a ruler. Humiliation and name calling were routine. The hairbrush was the prime weapon of choice for the callous women of God. For them Lucifer and hell were only hours away from their abandoned strays, and they felt an urgency to beat the goodness into our souls.

Five and a half years in the orphanage and nothing changed. Everyday was the same—the same food, the same clothes, the same bed, the same people. Sister Barbara, with thoughts of giving me a ray of hope, said to me the day we left, "Time changes everything. No matter how much we want things to be the same, they will never be the same. Life just keeps on moving forward, and so should you."

At the time I didn't know what Sister Barbara was talking about. I expected everything to be the same, even with my ma and pa. While my life in the orphanage had never changed, it had changed me forever. I just couldn't wait to get back to my ma and pa—to the life we had left behind five and a half years earlier. Little did I know that our idyllic life had gone out like the island tide.

The one thing that had not changed was my pa's drinking. I think he loved us, but he became very abusive toward both of us when soggy with drink. He rarely hit us, and his abuse was not as endless as that of the nuns. On the other hand, when he was drunk, which was most every weekend now that we were out of the orphanage, he was constantly on our backs about something. He never let up his screaming and yelling and threatening.

Sis finally took to stealing his crutches whenever he passed out. That way, when he awoke, he could only scream from the back bedroom. My pa screamed at my ma most of the time, too, whether he was drunk or not. Her health was no better. In fact, I think she was worse off in a lot of ways. She talked to herself even more, and my pa lost all patience with her.

My ma took to writing President Roosevelt about the poor condition our country was in due to the Depression. Not being able to afford stationery, she would write her letters on the insides of *Piggly Wiggly* grocery bags. She could fold a paper bag to look just like an envelope. With a stamp and return address it was ready for posting. We didn't know about the presidential letters until Bertha Kaiser, the mail lady, told me and Sis one day when we were picking up our mail

"Girls do y'all know yo' mama is writin' the president on paper bags from down at the *Piggly Wiggly*?" Mrs. Kaiser said, in her upcountry smokers voice.

"Ma'am?" we said together, because we only picked up on the words mama, president and *Piggly Wiggly*.

"Yeah," she giggled. "She writes letters to Roosevelt on grocery bags."

Sensing our embarrassment, she continued, "Now y'all don't be embarrassed. I know she ain't well from that sleeping sickness and what all else she has been through."

Sis told Mrs. Kaiser to keep the letters aside and we would pick them up when we picked up our regular mail.

"I can't do that, chile. That would be tamperin' with the US mail. If a letter has a stamp and an address, then I gotta send it. Yo mama folds the best envelopes I ever seen from grocery bags. She's like one of them oregoni folders. Why don't y'all just keep an eye on her and git them letters before she brings them to me?"

Sis decided not to tell my pa about my ma's letters to the president because it would just give him another reason to yell at her, but he found out anyway when he kept finding bits and pieces of *Piggly Wiggly* grocery bags in the garbage.

"Delia," my pa yelled. "Why in the hell are all these grocery bags being torn and thrown away?"

"I can't afford the stationery," was her logical response.

"What in hell do you need stationery for? You ain't got nobody to write. Everybody you know lives in Charleston."

"I have to write President Roosevelt," she responded, at about a third of the volume of his question.

"President damned Roosevelt? You mean you been writing the President of the United States on grocery bag paper from the *Piggly Wiggly*? Delia, what the hell have you been writing that son-of-a-bitch for?"

Ma answered in a very conversational tone, "Because he is the president. He can help."

"Help who? Help what? Hells bells, woman, have you gone slap loco? That man ain't got time to help you. He's got more than he can handle keeping up with that ugly wife of his and ruining this country. How in the world is he going to help us?"

Then, with more calm than before, my pa asked my ma, "Exactly what have you been saying in those letters?"

"I just tell him about our family. About how the girls were taken from us, and how you are crippled and can't get a job, and about how the chickens ain't been laying enough for me to get egg money. I tell him about how you drink…"

My pa interrupted her, "You told the president of the United States that I drink? Mary, mother of Jesus, woman, have you lost it all? Jesus. Jesus!"

"Listen, Delia," my pa said, trying to bring some serenity back into his voice. "I don't want you writing the president. I don't want you writing the vice president and certainly don't want you writing his ugly wife."

After a long moment, my pa said, "If those damned hens ain't laying enough eggs for you then I will buy some more damned chickens."

My ma didn't write Mr. Roosevelt any more letters after that, but she used to talk to him a lot. I would catch her on the porch talking.

"President Roosevelt, this country is in one mell of a hess, and you got to do something. I believe you can. I voted for you. Jessie didn't, though. He said your wife was too ugly. He said if a man would marry a woman that ugly, then there was no way he could make good decisions for this country. I disagree. Mrs. Roosevelt ain't that ugly. I know lots of uglier women. Take my aunt Katie. She ain't much prettier, which explains why she ain't never married."

The conversation moved on to chickens and my pa's lack of work. "I do wish you could help me with my chickens. They just won't lay like they should. I feed them good scratch, but it don't seem to help much. It might be the weather. It gets awfully hot on Sullivan's Island in the summertime. I know if I was a chicken, it would be way too hot for me to lay, but I don't suppose you can do much about the weather here in Charleston.

"And another thing, my husband, Jakey, ain't got no job. He's a good worker. He can paint houses, and he can cook. It just don't seem like anybody needs any help these days. Jakey is a cripple, too, but that don't stop him from being a hard worker. Why, he can go up a ladder as fast as any man with two good legs. It just seems like no one can afford to have their houses painted, whether it be by a one-legged man or a man with two good legs."

I never tried to stop my ma from talking to herself or to the president. Neither did Sis. Her talking to the president or to anyone else who didn't exist would irritate my pa, but he didn't try to stop her either, unless people were around.

Life on Sullivan's Island during the Depression years was as rote and routine as the years spent in the orphanage, especially for two who had recently escaped the inflexible demands of the Sisters of Charity. After Sis and I had been home for about a year or so our Pa got a job with the WPA or the PWA. I can't remember which. He was painting buildings at Fort Moultrie on the far end of Sullivan's Island. Sis told him he could thank our ma for the job since her letters to the president were responsible for his employment. He got red faced just thinking about those letters.

My pa also got red faced from having a steady job and a steady income and a steady supply of cheap booze. He started Friday evening after cashing his paycheck and steadily drank until Sunday morning. The only things about him that weren't steady were his hands and his one good leg.

I was becoming more and more afraid of my pa when he drank. I was sixteen years old but still small for my age. I didn't weigh ninety pounds with my pockets full of eggs, and I wasn't even tall enough to reach the upper bunk in the chicken coop. I was no match for my pa even if he were as blind drunk as an Irish pub crawler. Even though he never hit me with much starch, I was afraid that he would someday when he was drinking.

Meals for our Knight family were as monotonous as the brown *Piggly Wiggly* bags that my ma used as stationery. Greens, be they collards or turnips, were the only things of color to bolster an otherwise color-less plate. Every meal involved a fragment of chicken and a serving of white rice.

Sis and I looked forward to any holiday meal. Easter, Thanksgiving, and Christmas were the big three, but Thanksgiving trumped them all. It was a holiday about Pilgrims and Indians eating food and Americans replicating that feast of thanks.

The Thanksgiving meal of 1937 was the best. Pa had his paint money and allowed ma the luxury of treating his family.

The sweet memories of that Thanksgiving were short lived. On the Friday after Thanksgiving of 1937, while we dined on turkey scrapings and dressing leftovers, pa went into one of his rages. All of his anger was aimed at me. I had made the mistake of asking my pa if I could spend the weekend with Cousin Ellen. I used the excuse that I wanted to go to Sunday Mass with Ellen, thinking that a church service would soothe the thought of me being with my hated relatives on the main-land. In truth, I wanted an escape from my pa's weekend fury.

"You think you are better than the rest of us, don't you?" he began.

"No, Pa" I said, wishing I had never mentioned my cousin Ellen or Sunday Mass.

It began to build. "You are just like the whole lot over in Charleston. You got your nose stuck up in the air like you don't smell anybody else's shit. Let me remind you little missy—you ain't nothing but a Knight, just like the rest of us."

"Nothing but a Knight," my ma said to herself.

"Pa I won't go to Aunt Bridget's, and I don't have to go to Mass with Ellen."

"You're damned right you won't be going over there 'cause you are going to stay right here with your own damned family," he yelled.

"I want you to——" he started, but he was interrupted by Sis.

"Pa, leave Muff alone," she said, coming to my defense. Sis had come to my defense a lot over the past year, but my pa had not shown this much amplification before.

"You shut your feeder," he screamed at Sis, while at the same time picking up the turkey carving knife resting on the leftovers platter from Thanksgiving.

I bolted from the supper table, and in my haste to retreat, I ended up in the corner of the kitchen with no outlet for escape. My pa came reeling toward me, crutchless, with turkey carving knife in hand. I kept backing up, but with no where to go, I slid to the floor. My pa reached the corner and planted a hand on each wall, partly for balance but mostly to keep me pinned to the floor.

"You think you are better than the rest of us," he repeated. "I should just cut your throat like I should have done to your uncle Frank to put you both out of your misery," he continued, while waving the turkey knife as if he were in a sword fight with Errol Flynn.

Sis came up behind my pa, gently but with force. She grabbed his Captain Blood arm and then placed her free hand on his shoulder. "Pa, that's enough. You leave Muff alone now. Come on, let me put you to bed."

My pa melted. He usually did whenever Sis was forceful with him. She had some kind of hold over him that neither I nor my ma could muster. My pa put his arms around Sis's shoulders as she helped him to his bed. Sis also made sure she stole his crutch until he sobered up on Sunday.

It was surprising that my pa would allow me and Sis out of the house at all. He saw doom and danger in every dune on Sullivan's Island. Crossing Breach Inlet was like being ferried across that river in hell. Fortunately, he was usually passed out by Saturday night, so our liberation was without conflict.

Both Sis and I loved to dance, and we used every opportunity of my pa's Irishness to go to the Isle of Palms on Saturday night. The Isle of Palms was the place to be on Saturday night, with its inexplicable mixture of islanders, Charlestonians, vacationers, soldiers, and sailors. The Isle of Palms was like a county fair. The Ferris wheel, the focus of the amusements, was the largest I had ever seen, not that I had ever seen any. It was spider legged by a merry-go-round and any number of kiddie rides.

Sis and I didn't go to the Isle of Palms for the rides. Dancing was our inspiration. We were never lacking for dance partners with the naval base and army post nearby. We could dance all night, or at least until the ferry bell rang to usher the soldiers and sailors back to base.

Labor Day weekend of 1938 offered the final big dance of the summer season. The end-of-summer dance was one that Sis and I had not missed since our return home from the orphanage. This year was no different. Almost as soon as we arrived at the pavilion at the Isle of Palms, Sis and I both began to reconnoiter the dance floor for soldiers. *Reconnoiter* was a word we picked up from some private we had met back earlier in the summer. It seemed a proper fit for our scouting purposes.

The dance floor was crowded with uniformed Fred Astaire wannabes from all military branches and local Charleston girls with much the same designs as Sis and me.

No sooner had we arrived for our final fling for the summer than Sis and I spotted a soldier that sparked our interest. As was our practice, we would separate, scout the hall for dance partners, and meet back to divvy up our finds. Sis particularly liked sailors. I was partial to soldiers. However, on this occasion Sis became a land lubber. We settled this disagreement as we did all others—we counted potatoes. I won the potato count and I won the soldier.

I approached the private using a line that had worked so many times for me in the past. "You want a bite of my ice cream cone?"

He set down his Budweiser and dropped his half-smoked unfiltered Camel to the salt-weathered woodwork of the Isle of Palms pavilion, grinding the stub with the toe end of his shoe.

"Sure, I'd like to bite your ice cream cone," he said.

Overlooking his eagerness for biting my cone, I asked him, "What's your name?"

"John Billy Bailey."

"Well, John Billy Bailey, I hope you like chocolate."

John Billy Bailey wasn't much for dancing, but he did a splendid job of holding my cone while Sis and I laid down the moves that we had been practicing all summer. He managed to keep the chocolate drippings clear of his hands on both cones and was sticky-free when I returned from a hop.

Swing was in, and we managed our own tamed-down versions of the Lindy and the Charleston. Pa enjoyed watching us doing our at-home practicing, but we knew better than to get grody in public. At home, Pa would howl when we tried to teach Ma the Big Apple or the Black Bottom—two dances we shied away from at the pavilion.

I did manage to bully John Billy into a couple of slow dances. The live band that played all the big holiday promenades on the Isle of Palms, Sammy Scott and his Scotsmen, were agreeable to playing any request. They could play anything and make it sound just like Ted Lewis or Benny Goodman or Glenn Miller or Artie Shaw. I especially liked their version of "Cheek to Cheek". John Billy was no Fred Astaire, but I definitely felt like Ginger Rogers in his arms. There were no dips or turns, but we were cheek to cheek.

By the night's end I had John Billy in the corner, annoying him with attempts to master the fine craft of the fast dance, but my struggle was useless. "Tar Paper Stomp" was no more than just that, a stomp. In short order, we were back to "Once in a While" and "I'm Getting Sentimental Over You".

The music stopped at 11:30 to allow the military men enough time to catch the ferry or a bus and to get back to their stations. It was also enough time for me and Sis to meet our curfew of midnight. I no longer followed Sis blindly. In fact, I felt a need to audit her every move. She was still subject to making unsound decisions. She made one this night.

"Sis, we need to go," I suggested, knowing so well that she was in no mood to follow my advice.

"You go on. I'll catch a ride. I'll be right behind you," she said, while at the same time holding up an adequately drunken sailor.

"You need to come with me now," I said, but without any imposed urgency. That would have been useless.

"OK, I am leaving," I said. "Don't be stupid. You know Ma and Pa. They ain't gonna be pleased if you come home late."

"They'll get over it."

I made it home a few minutes of twelve. Pa had gone to bed, but Ma was up waiting.

"Where is your sister?" she asked, but without much annoyance.

"She was right behind me. The first bus was crowded so she took the other," I lied, and Ma knew it. She could always tell when I gave a slight stretch when it came to covering for Sis.

Ma locked the door at precisely twelve midnight. "Let's go to bed," she said.

"Sis should be here any second," I insisted, but, without any betrayal to Sis. I knew she was no where near Sullivan's Island.

I couldn't sleep. I heard Pa snoring. I knew Ma was wide awake. In what seemed like a coon's age, I heard Sis fiddling with the doorknob. It didn't take long before the demanding knocks began, followed by a commotion, an impatient protest of "Who locked this door?"

Locking doors was not something we did on Sullivan's Island. There was no need, and besides, an open door allowed for the ocean air to create a little cooling breeze.

My ma didn't stir for sometime, but Sis never gave up her protests. One by one the neighbor's porch lights began to blink. Ma relented, got up, and opened the door. Sis came storming in like a demon on assignment. "Who locked that door?" she demanded.

"You missed curfew," Ma said, as calmly as if she were talking to the priest at Easter.

"I missed my ride. Didn't Muff tell you?"

"She shouldn't be dishonest to protect you. It is not her nature to lie."

"She was raised by the same lying nuns as I was. She learned as well as anyone there how to be sneaky. You need to quit taking up for her," Sis shouted.

I heard the springs squeak as Pa stirred in his bed. I thought to myself, Sis is becoming just like our pa—hating the world and everyone in it. Everything and everyone was either the enemy or a threat, and Sis, like my pa, was determined to do battle with both.

Ma calmly tried to point out that Sis had to obey the house rules. The curfew had to be obeyed, mostly for her own safety. However, there was no reasoning with Sis. She felt grown and she felt determined to win this row. The urge to upgrade this imagined fray was out of her control. I could see it coming. I had seen it often enough in the orphanage. Words were not enough to satisfy. Sis needed wounds and scars. The fight was not over until someone raised the white flag of surrender.

"We'll talk in the morn," Ma said, still with little emotion.

"Like hell we will," Sis countered, at the same time slapping Ma across the face.

Sitting on ready, I impulsively made a blue streak to Sis. As soon as I grabbed her, I felt her energy fold up. No more fight was left. She lightly pushed me aside and went to bed.

Ma, sitting on the sofa by now, said, "Ain't she just like your pa."

Chapter 8

The Five-Day Courtship

I married John Billy Bailey on Friday. No romance. No engagement. No dating, unless you call walking on the beach sands of Sullivan's Island dating. I don't know why I did it. He could have been one of those cold-blooded serial killers we hear so much about. For all I knew, he could have been a thief, a philanderer, a hooligan, or a gangster. But he asked, and I said yes.

John Billy met my parents and Sis again on the day after the Labor Day dance. He just dropped by our rental at lunchtime unannounced. My pa was still sleeping off his Labor Day bender, and Ma was warming up the collards, beans, and rice. Sis was still sequestered in our room, embarrassed and trying to muster up the mettle to square things with Ma. My ma took an immediate liking to John Billy. She directed me to finish the food preparation while she received our guest.

"Come, lets go sit on the veranda," she said to John Billy, taking him by the hand and leading him to the porch. How our stoop became a veranda is beyond me.

"We can talk while Muff finishes lunch. You are staying for lunch, aren't you? Of course you are. So you are an army boy? How much longer do you have to serve?" she dug.

"I am being discharged on Thursday. I—"

Ma allowed him no opportunity to continue. "Where are you from? You don't talk like a Charlestonian. You threw an *r* in on your discharged. We don't much hanker to *r*'s in Charleston."

"I'm from Tallapoosa, Georgia."

"Say what? There is that *r* again. We say *Gawga*. Now where are you from again? I know about Savannah, but I don't know any *Talabooso*. Where is that? Is that Klan country?"

"It's Tal-la-poo-sa," John Billy said, draqging out each syllable of his hometown. "Tallapoosa is northwest of Atlanta, about forty miles."

"Now I've heard of Atlanta," Ma interrupted again. "I wouldn't want to live there. Georgia folks are mean, so I hear."

"Oh, we're not so mean," said John Billy.

"Time to eat." I thought it best that I interrupted the cross-examination before Ma got into politics or religion.

Ma took John Billy by the hand and led him to the kitchen table and seated him at the head, right next to her. About that time Pa stirred from his lair, sober but still red faced.

"You're in my seat," my pa said to John Billy with little curiosity about the stranger seated at his lunch table.

"Jakey, this is John Billy Bailey," my ma said, introducing John Billy. "He is from over at Fort Moultrie. He has dropped by for lunch."

"He's still in my seat."

"Oh, I'm sorry," John Billy apologized, as he got up to move next to me. "My daddy always sits at the head of the table back home. That's where the breadwinner of the family should be seated."

"Well, I didn't win much bread on this one, did I?"

"Looks good to me," John Billy offered. "It's just like what I would eat back home, except we'd have corn bread instead of rice, but rice is good. I've eaten a lot of rice since I've been stationed here."

Ma started serving. John Billy first, of course. Serving a guest for her was like talking. Once she got started, she couldn't seem to find a stopping point.

Pa stopped her. "If you don't stop stacking those beans, the boy is gonna have more gas than the gasbag Democrats running this state."

Just as I was about to admonish Pa for his gas remark, Sis dawdled in from our bedroom. She must have heard us talking because she had taken the time to smarten up her face. She moved to Ma with a penitent hug and a whispered, "I'm sorry." Ma patted Sis's arms but said nothing. My ma was a forgiving soul and not one to bear any malice.

Sis spoke few words. "Hello Johnny," were the only words she spoke to John Billy. I didn't bother to correct her on his name. She could brood on her own time.

After lunch John Billy and I strolled to the beach. I took the opportunity to apologize for my family.

"No need for an apology," he said. "You are not alone. A family is like a Baby Ruth—sweet, but always with a few nuts. Just remember, it don't matter how poor you are—if you have family, you are rich. Always be proud of your family. An ounce of blood is worth more than a ton of friendships."

We spent the afternoon on the beach, staring at the ocean. I took the time to tell John Billy about my aunts and the orphanage and my pa's drinking and anger, and about Sis's tussles with authority and her own self-control and about her slapping Ma. He listened without judgment—I could tell.

The following day we spent in Charleston. I showed John Billy the orphan's home on Queen Street. We picnicked at Battery Park, walked to the Market, and took a quick walk past my aunts' houses on Hasell Street. He couldn't believe Sis and I had walked the ledge on the Custom House.

Charleston at summer's end is a city of romance. It is surrounded by two gentle rivers and fronted by that magnificent ocean. Perhaps it is the Venetian isolation of the waters that creates the charm. Perhaps it is the wind pushing out the humid heat of summer and drawing in the tender mildness of the early fall. I don't know. Could it be the historic mansions that line the Battery with their prospect, real or imagined, of better days? Could it be the merry bells of Saint Michael's offering inspiration of hope and joy, along with an abandonment of the past and a settled vision of the future? No matter the inspiration, there was a blessing in the breeze for us both. The parks, the cemeteries, and the urban gardens all pitched in to awaken a sleeping passion for lost love that I felt in the belly of my heart.

Evidently, John Billy felt the same stirring. "Let's get married," he said as we walked along East Bay Street back toward Battery Park. We were right in front of the row of homes famously known today as Rainbow Row. In 1939, these old warehouses, stores, and upstairs homes were still in disrepair but were beginning to see some renovation. When I was growing up, this area of Charleston was rather seedy, not a place you would stray unless you were two little girls skipping school and looking for an adventure.

"Married? What for?" I asked.

"Well, I think I love you," John Billy said, but with little certainty about his conviction.

"You know I am only seventeen."

"So what? Plenty of girls marry younger than seventeen back where I come from. I know a girl who got married at twelve. She was having babies a year later," he said, trying to lighten my fears.

"You'll have to ask my ma and pa," I said to him, hoping to perhaps dissuade while I gave this jaw-dropper more thought.

"OK. Let's go ask them."

Not a word was said during the bus ride back to Sullivan's Island. I was into my own thoughts. How were Ma and Pa going to accept this? They would never consent. Who was this character? My pa would stab him.

On the way from the bus stop to Ma and Pa's John Billy said, "Don't worry. I will take care of this. Everything is going to be OK."

Ma and Pa were listening to the radio when we entered my house. A radio ad for 20 Mule Team Borax was playing. I turned the radio down and said, "Ma and Pa, can we talk to you a second?"

John Billy took over. "Mr. and Mrs. Knight, Mary Margaret and I are getting married. We want your blessing."

"OK," my pa said. "Now will you turn the damn radio back up?"

My ma was a bit more curious. With clarity, she asked, "Where are y'all going to live? John Billy, you are getting out of the army. Do you have a job lined up?"

"We are going to Georgia for a couple of weeks so Mary Margaret can meet my parents and brothers and sisters. Then we will come back here, and I will find a job and us a home."

"We are going to Georgia?" I whispered in total shock. It was not something we had discussed. I was to find out quickly that discussing things was not one of John Billy's strong suits.

Sis had her nose stuck in a recent edition of *Movie Mirror*. Taking time from an article on why Cary Grant could not stay in love, she looked up to ask, "Where are you two going to get married?"

"Right here. I'll get a justice of the peace or my army chaplain to come over. I'll be discharged in the morning. We'll do it tomorrow evening. We will be leaving for Tallapoosa Saturday morning."

I could tell by the look on her face and the tone of her voice that Sis was troubled. The green-eyed monster of envy was riding her hard, as well as the prospect that she was to be left alone with Ma and Pa. As she returned to her *Movie Mirror* she said, "I hope you have better luck than Cary Grant."

As for me, I guess I just wanted to get away—away from my pa, away from my memories of the orphanage, and away from the tedium of my life's routine. So marrying John Billy Bailey just seemed like the right thing to do at the time.

"We are going to Georgia?" I asked John Billy after kissing him goodbye for the night. "I've never been out of Charleston."

"Well, it's about time you saw the world. Tallapoosa will be a good start."

TALLAPOOSA, GEORGIA, 1938

Chapter 9

Midnight Bane to Georgia

A church wedding was out of the question. I was a Catholic, and John Billy was a Baptist of some kind. I guess I was removed from the church because I married out of my faith. None of my aunts came to the wedding, even though Ma had invited them. I suppose they disowned me because I was marrying a non-Catholic. My ma and pa and Sis were there, and two of my island friends, Vera Ponti and Gladys Snowden. We did marry in my parents' home, which was in fact Uncle Frank's house. It was a civil ceremony with a justice of the peace.

We spent the night in the Francis Marion Hotel, which was a source of great satisfaction for me. As a child growing up in Charleston I could only daydream about escaping to such a luxurious palace. It would have been a Cinderella fantasy for me, since I was a child of Charleston's most needy.

John Billy had borrowed a 1935 Ford from Alton Cook. Alton had also attended our wedding. Alton was an army buddy with a heart of gold. Alton was from Soddy Daisy, Tennessee. Alton's folks had means, and they furnished him with a car once he returned from Panama. He had another six months of duty left, and since he was to be stuck at Fort Moultrie for the duration, he had no immediate need for transportation. He made the offer of his Ford as a wedding gift. We were ever thankful.

"Lord, bless this food we are about to receive," John Billy said, blessing our first breakfast together.

"What was that? I mean, where did you learn that?" I asked, surprised that he prayed at breakfast. My pa never blessed our food. Ma would pray to herself and make the sign of the cross, but she was never one to put her religion on display. She quoted Jesus. "When you pray, do not be like the hypocrites, for they love to pray standing in the churches and on the street corners to be seen by others."

John Billy explained, "That was the blessing my daddy always said before each meal. There was no eating until he uttered those words. He said no more and no less. He is a man of unyielding habits. His daily routine has little variety. He wakes the same time every day. He eats the same breakfast every morning, right after he blesses his food with that prayer—two fried eggs, corn grits, salted ham, homemade biscuits with butter and cane syrup, and coffee, black. For lunch he has whatever vegetables are in season and a glass of buttermilk and cornbread. On Sunday he adds chicken to his fare. For supper he has leftover vegetables from lunch with some cut of pork. Immediately after each meal, he places in his mouth a uniform wad of his favorite tobacco—Beechnut."

I was looking forward to the drive to Tallapoosa, for the opportunity to get to know John Billy, my husband whom I knew absolutely nothing about. Once we proceeded to Highway 78, I began to ask John Billy about his family and his life.

"Tell me about your mother. What is she like?"

"My mama—her name is Sarah, I don't think she is a happy woman. Sometimes she has to fear the wrath of my daddy, who always seems to be angry about something. She always says 'amen' to his boring, repetitive prayers. The nine of us, the children that is, were most often blind to our daddy's rigid habits and our mama's fears. We were forever having to be reminded to echo Mama's 'amens'."

"'You boys give an *amen* to your daddy's blessing,' she would command, ignoring my three sisters, just like my daddy had ignored her for as long as I could remember. Yeah, my mama was accustomed to being ignored by Daddy, just as she had become accustomed to being called 'Miss' in spite of the fact that she had been married all those years. She was burdened with carrying that moniker because she had waited until, as they say, 'late in life' to marry. I think she knew that Daddy did not love her. She knew that Daddy only married her for three reasons—to tend to his twin babies, to keep his house, and to have as many sons as possible."

"He had twin babies when they married?"

"Yes, he had a first wife. She died when birthing the twins. They also had three older sons who are my half brothers, but they are up and gone now. When Daddy proposed to my mama she felt obligated. For her time was running out. I think she was twenty-seven or so. He was approaching forty. But anyway, he proposed and she accepted. Her mother encouraged it, thinking my daddy was a man of some means because he owned a horse and a buggy. By the time they got married, the title of 'Miss' had already become as much a part of her as the single-haired mole on her chin."

"For us, mealtime was about as boring as Daddy's mealtime blessings. Daddy expected total silence with an allowed exception to ask for seconds. The request for seconds had to be escorted by a 'please.' No one dared respond to a simple request to pass the potatoes. To do so would have incurred the wrath of Daddy or Mama, and a slap to the noggin was sure to follow."

"Is your daddy a mean man?" I interrupted.

"Not to everyone, and not all the time. Over time, I learned to avoid Daddy's rage when it flared. We all did. Too many times in the past I had become the victim of his uncontrolled temper. Talmage—that's my brother next to me in age—he never seemed to learn or just couldn't resist the temptation to arouse Daddy's passionate side."

"Talmage had a slight stutter when he spoke, but he would exaggerate it just to gnaw at Daddy. I remember at one meal Talmage caused a ruckus. He said to me, 'Pppass the pppeas.'

"'What did you say, young man?' Daddy said, giving Talmage a second chance to amend his request for peas before he smacked his head.

"'Oh, excuse mmme. I mmmeant to say 'pppass the ppplease pppeas,'" Talmage stuttered.

"'That's more like it,' Daddy said while passing the black-eyes and totally missing Talmage's teasing word reversal.

"Talmage wasn't hungry for more peas. He had filled up on greens and chicken and had no room in his belly for a single pea. He just wanted to see how far he could get with Daddy before he caused an explosion.

"Since Daddy had missed Talmage's pea ploy, Talmage felt full of himself. Keeping his eye on Daddy, he waited for the opportune time when Daddy was distracted while slurping his buttermilk and corn bread. Talmage placed a black-eyed pea in the cup of his spoon and flipped the pea at me.

"I scraped the pea off the bib of my overalls and gave Talmage a look to suggest that he was taking things too far. My look did nothing for Talmage except to challenge his daring. The second pea was in my hair.

"'Cut it out, Talmage,' I said softly, but loud enough so that Daddy stopped in mid-gulp of corn bread and buttermilk to glare at us both.

"When the third pea missed me, I had had enough of Talmage's nonsense. I knew he wouldn't stop until Daddy was provoked. I had seen Talmage incite Daddy before, and we all had to suffer. He had to be stopped. So without any thought to consequences, I picked up my fork and slung it at Talmage. The fork stuck in the meaty part of his cheek, just below the left eye. Briefly, and just before Talmage could reach for his fork to retaliate, I watched my fork quiver in his cheek. Just as quickly, I felt Daddy's hand lock into the bib strap of my overalls right near where the pea had stained the denim. With his other hand, the one he was using to cut up his cornbread to add more to his butter-milk, he hit me across the side of the neck. I could feel the knife stinging my ear. At the first trickle of blood, Daddy dropped the knife, but he continued to slap me until the screams of Talmage drew his attention.

"'I'm blind! I'm blind!' Talmage screamed, with no stutter at all.

"When Daddy let go of my overalls' strap, I fell to the floor and crawled under the table, seeking refuge from the kicks that I expected to follow. They would have followed too, except Talmage's screams redirected Daddy's interest."

"'Move, woman,' Daddy ordered Mama. Mama had immediately gone to Talmage's aid. 'Let me take a look at the boy.' Talmage didn't resist.

"'You ain't blind, boy,' Daddy stated in a strange calmness rather than the expected rage.

"Daddy gently removed the fork from Talmage's cheek. After inspecting the four slightly bleeding pockmarks in Talmage's face, he turned to Mama and gave his usual postmeal order. 'You girls clean off the table'. Looking at me he said, 'You boys have some work to do, I believe.'

"I crawled out from under the table on the opposite side from where Daddy and Talmage were by now standing and nearer to the kitchen door, which was the quickest exit from the house. My little brothers, Paul and Talmage followed my swift departure."

"After we got out of hearing distance of Daddy, Talmage said to Paul, 'Where do you think you are going, mule-turd breath?' Talmage always took his frustrations out on our little brother.

"'I'm going to feed my chicken,' Paul replied, ignoring Talmage's reference to his breath odor.

"'We had your chicken for supper tonight. I wrung his neck this afternoon,' Talmage continued his taunt, hoping to make Paul cry.

"'You're a fat lie,' Paul said, his voice quivering as tears began to well up in his eyes.

"I said to Talmage, 'Leave him alone. He's not hurting anyone.'

"Talmage dared not push me too far, especially when we were out of sight of Mama and Daddy. He knew I had a temper and that I would explode with little provocation. I was like Daddy in that regard. He had just witnessed that at the table, as he had many times in the past. Even though he was almost my size, Talmage didn't wish to challenge me. He had once when we lived back in Powder Springs, Georgia. I dragged him from the barn to the henhouse and rubbed his nose in chicken litter until he cried.

"'Yyyou just like the ooold mmman,' he cried, while wiping chicken poop from his face."

Chapter 10

Georgia Crackers

John Billy and I stopped near Augusta for a bite to eat. His chronicled conversation came to a freeze while I explored my first nibble of a Georgia blue plate special—potato salad, green beans, fried chicken, buttered corn bread muffins, and sweet tea. Of course, the meal was graced with his pa's colorless blessing. After our noon repast, we were back on Highway 78 traversing the red hills of Georgia toward Tallapoosa.

"How did your ma and pa get together? Have they always lived in Tallapoosa?" I asked. After the morning drive's conversation, I knew I only needed to stimulate John Billy's remembrances to initiate a glut of flashbacks from his growing up in Georgia.

"Daddy was born in Henry County, just south of Atlanta. He comes from a family with a history of rambling. Wherever they were, they wanted to be somewhere else; they were always searching for a vision of the picture-perfect farm. My great-grandfather and great-grandmother both came from South Carolina and settled a short while in this part of Georgia—Oglethorpe County, I think. They then moved on to Henry County and raised thirteen children. The Civil War came along and snatched up most of the boys. After the war, the older sons scattered across Georgia. One son, who was attending a medical school here in Augusta when the war broke out, ended up in the medical corps for the rebel army. One family story says that early in the war, he leaned his rifle up against a tree and left it there. He decided he was just going to treat the wounded—no matter which side they were fighting for. He spent the remainder of the war tending the sick and wounded, including the Yankees. After the war he was headed to Missouri but got sidetracked in the Sand Mountain region of Alabama and set up a practice there. I don't think he ever went back to school to formalize his status as a full-fledged doctor, but his battlefield experience certainly qualified him."

John Billy continued his saga about places that were foreign to me. "My grandfather moved to Walton County after the war. He and his wife raised ten children including my daddy. Daddy married a lady named Smith, and they had five children including the twin girls. Mrs. Smith, as I told you, died giving birth to the girls. One of Daddy's sisters helped with the girls at first, but it wasn't but a short time before my daddy found my mama. She was available, and he needed a helpmate. Mama and Daddy, when they got married, lived in Loganville which was right on the Gwinnett County and Walton County line. We'll pass through there shortly.

"Daddy was not only a farmer but also a man of many callings. He had attended a small institute in Auburn, Georgia. He became a surveyor and a justice of the peace, and once we all were old enough to work his farm, he became a schoolteacher. He did anything he could do to supplement his meager earnings from his farming.

"All nine of us were born in Loganville, but it wasn't long before Daddy got the itch to find that better farm. Being a surveyor afforded him the opportunity to scout out farms on the market. He located a farm in Powder Springs, Georgia, that was ten acres larger than the one we had in Loganville. That lasted about two growing seasons. He was then offered a job teaching school in Tallapoosa for eight months out of the year. With eight children and a wife, he had plenty of hands to help man the farm while he was at school. Today the farm is lying fallow for the most part. He has a vegetable garden and a cow and some chickens, and he usually has a goat for fall slaughter. Paul is still around, but like my half brothers and me, he will be gone as soon as he reaches eighteen.

"Today, Daddy pretty much sits on the porch and watches Paul and whatever seasonal jobber he can recruit and the colored family that lives on our farm do the manual labor—milking, hoeing, plowing. He is the overseer who just sits chewing his Beechnut chewing tobacco and missing the brass spittoon as often as not."

"When you were home, did you and the brothers do anything besides work?" I asked, wanting to learn more about the man I had married merely a day prior.

"Daddy would call Paul in at dark but allowed me and Talmage the freedom to explore. It was the only playtime we had. During the school season, we worked from the time we arrived home until supper. After supper, we did chores until dark. When we were not in school, we worked all day."

"What did you do for fun?" I interrupted.

"Well, I'm not sure you would call it fun," John Billy said with a laugh.

"One night after we had finished our chores, Talmage said to me, 'Let's Panic the Posts.'

"'Are you crazy? I asked, knowing that Talmage was bent on his devilish mischief."

"'Aw, the ooold mmman is done for the nnnight. He's taken Pppaul inside. He don't ever come out here after sssupper.'

"Talmage took off running down the cow trail. I knew I couldn't go back to the house without him. Besides, I didn't want to go inside until bedtime. I started after Talmage. He ran like a rabbit being chased by a pack of beagles. Running was one thing Talmage could do better than me. Even with the near-full moon, and knowing I could run the cow trail blindfolded, it was all I could do to keep him in my line of sight. I'm sure he slowed a bit to allow me to catch up with him.

"'Panic the Posts' was something that Talmage and I did with some regularity in the summer. Talmage hated the colored. I could take them or leave them. If they didn't bother me, then I had no call to mess with them unless we were playing our game. I once asked Talmage why he hated the coloreds.

"''Cause they're nnniggers,'" he replied. For Talmage, it was all the reasoning he needed.

"There was a colored family that lived on our farm—Lazelle Post and his wife, Hazel. They had a bunch of kids, but the only one I knew was Broomstick Claude. All the Post children were skinny. Claude had picked up the nickname Broomstick years back. Sometimes I would shoot marbles with him on Sundays. Talmage wouldn't shoot with us.

"You couldn't ask for better neighbors. Lazelle often helped Daddy with picking and plowing and at hog-killing time. Daddy often said that there wasn't a better man at handling a headstrong mule than Lazelle Post, and there was no better cook in west Georgia than Hazel. Often, after Broomstick Claude took all my best marbles, Hazel would treat us to fried pork chops and collards. No one made collards better than Hazel Post."

"For all I know, the Posts were the only colored family in Haralson County. Daddy allowed the Post family to live on our land for free in exchange for the help that Lazelle gave him and for Hazel helping

Mama do her canning and preserving. They lived in a rickety wooden shanty about a mile from our farmhouse. Daddy volunteered an acre of land to Lazelle for their vegetable garden and gave him some of the hog parts after a hog killing. Often it was the parts of the hog Daddy didn't particularly fancy, like the jowls, the feet for pickling, and the intestines for chitlins."

"When I finally caught up with Talmage, he was waiting for me at the wild plum orchard about a hundred yards from the Posts' shack. The wild plum orchard was out of scent range of the mange-covered mongrels that slept under the stacked-rock-supported porch. Giving me time to catch my breath, Talmage whispered,'Wwhere does Lazzzelle get enough fffood to ffeed those mmmutts?'

"'They look like they get more to eat than that litter of whelps he calls "chilrens". Broomstick Claude is about as bony as pine sapling.' I whispered back.

"The game of 'Panic the Posts' was invented by Talmage shortly after Daddy began to let us stay outside after our evening chores. Part one was to see how close we could get to Lazelle Post's house without arousing his porch dogs. The second part of the game, the part that took the most skill, was to see if we could throw a rock between the cracks in the walls of the house. I don't think I ever was able to do it, but Talmage was the best rock thrower in all of Tallapoosa. I once saw him knock a blue jay off a fence post, and he rarely hunted rabbits or squirrels with his rifle.

"Since it was dark, we couldn't see our rocks go through the holes, but as Talmage always said, 'Yyyou know you hit a bbbullseye, if you hear a colored bbbaby ccry.'

"Talmage would fill his coverall pockets with choice throwing rocks he had picked out near the creek we had to cross to get to the Posts' house. I, on the other hand, would simply pick up rocks as we belly-crawled out of the wild plum orchard toward the target. As soon as we got to within chunking distance, Talmage stood up and let one of his flat creek rocks fly.

"'Aoowwww!'"

"'Bullseye!'" Talmage shouted, without stuttering and at the same time waking the wormy pack of mangy hounds settled under Lazelle Post's porch.

"'Let's get out of here,'" I screamed.

"Talmage caught and passed me about halfway back to the wild plum orchard. A black-and-tan mongrel caught me at about the same time Talmage was passing me. She sank her canines into my leg just below the calf muscle. I managed to shake her loose from my leg, but her teeth were hung up in my overalls. I fell to the ground trying to shake that bitch from my britches leg. Talmage heard my screams. He turned back in full gallop and began to launch a revolver of rocks my way. Throwing while in full stride diminished Talmage's precision. The first rock hit me square in the back.

"'You fool. Get this dog off me,' I shouted at Talmage.

"Talmage stopped running, took aim and hit the black-and-tan square in the head, knocking her loose from my pant leg and sending her back to her pack to again collapse under the Posts' porch.

"I lay limp for several minutes measuring the pain from the dog bite and from the rock that Talmage had so accurately plunked into the small of my back.

"I picked myself up from the ground, looked Talmage in the eye, and said, 'Thanks.'

"'Thhhat's what you get for stabbing me in the eye with the ffork.'"

Chapter 11

Spare the Rod; Spoil the Child

After leaving Augusta we eventually passed through Athens, Georgia, the home of the state university. I asked John Billy to ride through the campus since I had never seen a university before. I discovered very quickly that he was not one to veer off course when he had a destination in mind. Reluctantly, we made a drive-by. My fascination was with the young kids, most my age, promenading the campus grounds—full of smiles and ambition. I, on then other hand, was a married seventeen-year-old with a seventh grade education on my way to Tallapoosa, Georgia, to meet what sounded like a family as afflicted as my own.

Georgia towns have very peculiar names. Tallapoosa, John Billy told me, was a Creek Indian word for "grandmother town" because it was central to the Creek Indians who traipsed up and down the Tallapoosa River. The Creeks, he said, were the predominant tribe in west Georgia and Alabama. When white men first began to settle the area on the

Tallapoosa River, they traded with the Creeks for skins and even kid-napped Florida Indians to sell to other whites as slaves. Once the white man was entrenched in Alabama, the Creeks, by several dubious treaties, were forced from their homes. Ultimately, like the Cherokees, they were forced to relocate to the Indian Territory.

Between Athens and Loganville we passed through Between, Georgia. John Billy said Between was called Between because it was halfway between Loganville and Monroe, another town along our route. I wondered if Tallapoosa would be any bigger than the tiny town Between.

"Is Tallapoosa any larger than Between?" I asked John Billy.

"Oh, much larger. Between only has about a hundred residents. Tallapoosa has a couple of thousand."

He went on to explain that Tallapoosa was a gold-mining city and that's probably why the Indians were forced to leave west Georgia. Then, after the Civil War, a bunch of carpetbagging Yankees came down and set up several industries, the most lucrative being vineyards and wineries. Newly arrived Europeans in the north were encouraged to come to Tallapoosa to work the vineyards and make the wine. Many came from Hungary, but they came from all over Europe where wine was made. Eventually, the Georgia legislature passed a Prohibition law, and the wine industry was squeezed out of business. Throughout all this time, farming was big business, and, of course, with the railroad coming through, Tallapoosa remained an active small town.

As we approached Loganville, John Billy's birthplace, I gave up on trying to get him to do a drive-through to show me where he and his brothers and sisters were born. I settled for getting him back to telling me about his family and his growing up in Tallapoosa. He was quick to restart his story.

"I didn't sleep well," he said, returning to his story about Talmage saving him from the Post's family dogs, "from the dog bite and the bruising pain from Talmage's river rock. Early the next morning we got our wake-up call."

"'John Billy. Talmage. Time to get up,' Mama called from the bottom of the stairs.

"'Yes, ma'am,' Talmage answered. Talmage was an early riser. Always has been.

"I tried to roll out of bed, but the pain in my back and leg forced me to lie still.

"Talmage, fully dressed and headed down the stairs called back to me, 'John Billy, you better shake a leg.'

"'John Billy,' Mama called again. 'Did you hear me call you?'

"'Yes, ma'am. I heard you.' I answered with a surly tone to my voice.

"I rolled through the pain and managed to get both feet on the floor. I slowly managed to slip both of my feet through the pant legs of my overalls. As I pulled on my brogans, I heard Daddy's voice from the bottom of the stairs.

"'Son, your mama has done called you twice, and she's got more important things to do this morning than to spend all her time getting you out of bed. Get up. Now!'

"I heard Daddy's footsteps on the stairs as he headed up to roust me from my roost. I immediately stood up without bothering to lace my brogans and pulled my overalls up to my waist. Holding my overall straps in one hand and protecting my head with the other, bracing for the cuff that was sure to come, I ran past Daddy, who was by this time midway up the stairs. His left hand skimmed off my arm that was protecting my head. I was two steps below him when his right foot caught me in the small of my back, just inches from where Talmage had bruised me the night before with his errant rock. I held back a holler and tears, jumped the last five steps, and bolted out the front door, tripping over my unlaced brogans and falling down the steps leading off the front porch.

"I could never understand my daddy. How could he be so enraged one minute and so indifferent the next?

"Talmage was milking Bessie when I reached the barn.

"'Did you sleep well, John Billy?' he asked, smiling.

"'Kiss my ass,' I snapped at him.

"'Will that make it feel better?' he asked as his grin grew to the size of Bessie's milk-filled udders.

"After we had finished our chores, and after breakfast, we all piled into Daddy's 1928 Model A Ford to go to school. Daddy had purchased the car for, as he liked to say, 'a mule, a horse, a cow and some cash.'

"We all attended the same school. The Tallapoosa Grammar School had grades one through seven. I was in the seventh grade. Talmage was in the fifth, and Paul was in the second. The twins, Iola and Viola had completed the seventh grade and stayed home with Mama to work the farm until we boys got home from school.

"Daddy was the only teacher at the Tallapoosa Grammar School. He taught reading, spelling, penmanship, composition, history, geography, and arithmetic mostly. Me and the other older boys helped the little ones with their numbers and ABCs. Daddy was a strict teacher. He took no guff. The classroom was, generally, as quiet as our dinner table."

"Leviticus Phagan, Jr was the only boy to give Daddy a hard time. He didn't like being called Leviticus. His parents and my daddy called him Junior. The rest of us called him Deadeye, not because he was a marksman, but because his left eye drooped from a run-in he'd had with a guinea fowl he was chasing for sport. Deadeye was the oldest of the seventh graders by at least two years. He came for schooling so he wouldn't have to work his daddy's pulp wood business and paltry farm. We didn't see him much in the wintertime because there was little work to do on his daddy's farm during the fallow season. That also explains why he was yet in the seventh grade.

"Even though it was early March, it was still cold enough to burn stove wood to heat the schoolroom. Daddy always assigned one of the older boys the chore of starting the fire before the school day began.

"'Junior, go get some kindling for the stove,' Daddy ordered as soon as we arrived at school."

"'Yes, sir, Mr. Bailey,' Dead Eye responded, squinting through his one droopy eye.'

"When Deadeye returned from the woodshed, Daddy had already started the lesson on an arithmetic assignment. Daddy always started the day off with arithmetic. He said the brain was fresher then, and arithmetic needed a fresh brain. As Daddy was focused on helping the third graders cipher a troublesome arithmetic problem, Deadeye toyed with the woodstove in the center of the room, which was a distraction to the third graders. Deadeye started the fire easily enough, but since his mind was never fresh, he had no desire to begin his arithmetic assignment.

"As Daddy was helping Ezeke Putman with his subtraction, Deadeye began to make faces behind Daddy's back. Talmage was the first to notice and brought it to my attention by poking me in my rock-bruised back. I turned around to slap Talmage, but he diverted my attention by nodding toward Deadeye's contorted face.

"Talmage and I both knew that Deadeye was about to overstep the bounds of sober behavior. I looked at Deadeye to give him a head-shake warning, but he had both his bad eye and good eye squinting and his mouth gaping open like the mouth of a dog stuck with porcupine quills. Even if he had seen my tip-off to stop his foolery, I am sure he would have ignored me. So I decided to let him play it out.

"Talmage began to laugh. He put his head down on his desk to muffle his uncontrollable giggles, but his titters only served to bring the attention of the entire Tallapoosa Grammar School to Deadeye Phagan.

"Daddy stood up. As he looked at the class with a scowl, he reached into the woodbin for a log—a log that Deadeye should have been placing in the woodstove. Daddy spun around, and with one clean stroke, he caught Deadeye in mid-grimace. Deadeye hit the sawdust-covered floor before Daddy could catch him with a second swing of the hickory log.

"'Draw me some water, son,' Daddy said to Talmage, who had by now stopped his giggles.

"By the time Talmage had returned with the water, Deadeye's good eye was as tightly shut as his bad one. Daddy poured the entire bucket of water in Deadeye's face and then plucked Deadeye up from the floor. He looked Deadeye square in the eyelids and ordered him to leave Tallapoosa Grammar School and never return.

"Daddy, after delivering Deadeye to his feet and driving him out the door with a quick kick to his keister, turned back to the class and said, 'Ezeke Putman, do you know how to subtract yet?'

"When school let out for the afternoon, Deadeye Phagan and his daddy were waiting beside Daddy's Ford."

"'Did you do this to my boy, Mr. Bailey?' Mr. Phagan asked my daddy."

"Daddy, before answering Mr. Phagan, turned to me and said, 'John Billy, go get that piece of wood from the wood bin.' I knew which piece of wood he wanted.

"When I returned from the schoolhouse, Daddy and Mr. Phagan were nose to nose, but neither was saying a word. I handed Daddy the log that he had used to shut the good eye of Deadeye Phagan.

"Daddy, without blinking, said to Mr. Phagan, 'Do you see your son's face?'

"'Yeah, I see it,' came his peevish reply.'

"'Do you see this log?' my daddy asked him."

"'Yeah, I see it,' Mr. Phagan said, with even more ill-tempered irritation.

"'Well, sir,' Daddy said, with very little fire in his voice. 'If you first don't get your foot off my automobile and second don't get off these school grounds, I'm going to take this log and beat you with it so that you will be uglier than your boy there.'

"Mr. Phagan hesitated, looked again at his son and then took a second gander at the log. 'Well, Mr. Bailey, I'm not going to let you teach my boy again.'

"'Mr. Phagan, thank you,' my daddy said, as Mr. Phagan walked away with Deadeye. 'I haven't been able to teach Junior anything anyway.'

"I was proud of my daddy. He stood up to the school bully, and he stood up to the school's bully of a father. At the same time, I learned to fear him even more. He could have killed Deadeye in that one moment of uncontrolled anger, just as I had often thought he could have killed Talmage or me. I vowed then and there that I would never again be prey to one of his uncontrolled, venomous attacks."

Chapter 12

Meet the Parents

"I think I am afraid of your Pa," I said to John Billy just as we were passing Stone Mountain. He had told me to be on the lookout for the mountain. He had told me all about it, in between his stories of growing up in Tallapoosa. Stone Mountain was a massive outcropping of granite just outside Atlanta. In Charleston, we had no mountains of any kind. Everything was as flat as a back-beach flounder. Stone Mountain was strikingly large and bare of trees. It appeared that someone had chopped off the front face of the mountain. John Billy said they were planning a memorial to the Southern soldiers with a carving. He also said we were in Klan country. Stone Mountain, he said, had become the unofficial home to the Klan in Georgia.

"They burn crosses on top of the mountain, and don't worry about my dad," John Billy said. "He will treat you like a queen."

After we passed Stone Mountain, we began to approach Atlanta. Druid Hills must have been where the wealth of the city lived. The homes were imposing. We have beautiful homes in Charleston, but we have no grounds unless you would venture out toward the Ashley River.

Not far along past Druid Hills, John Billy said, "That's where the Crackers play."

I was looking at the towering building on my left, so his statement about crackers made no sense to me. "What kind of crackers?" I asked, thinking that the building I was looking at was where they made crackers.

"No, that's Sears Roebuck. Over there, to your right, the roof," he said, as he pointed to a baseball park. "That's where the Atlanta Crackers play. That's Atlanta's baseball team."

"They have a baseball team called the Crackers? Why would they name a team after a cracker?"

"Not a *cracker* cracker," he laughed. "'Cracker' is a nickname for people from Georgia. They say that the name came from south Georgia cattle farmers who drove their cattle into Florida to graze during the winter. They used bull whips to keep the cattle in line. The Florida folks were impressed with the Georgians and their ability to use the bullwhips and started calling them crackers. The name stuck, I guess, meaning anyone from Georgia.

"Babe Ruth once hit a ball that got stuck in the magnolia tree in center field," John Billy said with a degree of excitement.

"I don't know what you are taking about... candy bars, magnolia trees, crackers."

With that, John Billy pulled into the parking lot of the Atlanta Cracker's baseball team. The gates were locked, but with a bit of exploring, we made our way toward a railway overpass and scaled just enough for me to see the magnolia tree. While we, or at least John Billy, were marveling at the magnificent magnolia, John Billy told me that Babe Ruth once hit a 742-mile home run out of this park. I didn't know much about baseball, but I did know that no one could hit a baseball for miles, not even a country mile.

"What's the catch?" I asked.

"There was no catch," he said. "That's why the ball went 742 miles. He hesitated to allow his little leg-pull to simmer, and then he explained. "They say that the Babe hit one into a boxcar on the railroad tracks up there. When the train got to Missouri, someone found the ball still in the boxcar."

As we were making our way back to the car, I asked, "Do you believe that about Babe Ruth?"

"I don't know. Baseball is a funny game. I guess anything is possible."

From the ballpark we continued west on Highway 78, past the Georgia Institute of Technology and then past the Coca-Cola Company. We just looked and rode past. John Billy was eager to get out of Atlanta, and I was eager to hear more about his family.

He told me about his three half brothers. All had moved out as soon as they were of age. The oldest worked in a cotton mill in Cedartown, Georgia. The middle brother had moved up north to work in the steel mills and the youngest was working in Atlanta. His twin sisters were still in Tallapoosa. Each had married a local farm boy. Talmage had recently joined the army. Paul was still home, helping with the farm, but planned to join the navy as soon as he turned eighteen.

John Billy also told me about another brother of his who had died at the age of two. It seems that his ma took the boy out to the fields in a wagon when she was working there. One day, he picked up a rock and put it in his mouth. It got caught in his esophagus. His ma managed to dislodge it, but the boy, Newton, came down with pneumonia and died a few months later.

After covering the death of Newton, the conversation turned to religion.

"You will see. Daddy and Mama are bona fide believers. They are foot-washing, note-singing, Hard-Shell Baptists. I think that's where they get their 'spare the rod, spoil the child' approach to child rearing," John Billy said.

"I've never heard of a Hard-Shell Baptist. What do they believe?" I asked.

"Mostly what everyone else believes, but maybe a little more strict in the interpretation. They are sometimes called Primitive Baptists. They reject any formal services outside the church, so they don't do missions or seminaries because they think those are the work of men and not from God's teaching. They are also anti-Mason. They don't use pianos, and their singing is a cappella because there is nothing in the New Testament about instruments—just singing. They don't do Sunday school because they think it is the parents' job to instruct children in religion. Since Jesus and the apostles didn't go to seminaries to learn to preach, they see no need to sanction places to teach you how to preach. They also practice foot washing. They think that is a way to display community service and humility to members of the congregation, and it is a means of assuring equality in the church rather than rank."

"Catholics wash feet during Holy Week, before Easter. We have a pretty strict religion too. We do have a hierarchy, though, starting with the pope and the cardinals down to the priest and nuns. I think that is because Jesus told Peter he was the rock on which the church would be built, so Peter became the first pope. We are a little more serious about the Last Supper and the bread and wine being the body and blood of Christ. Mary has a special place in the Catholic church. She is a role model for all women through her servitude," I said, giving Billy a quick outline of the Catholic religion.

"Well, I guess they all have a common goal—be good, be good to others and live the best you can and try to get into heaven. All the other stuff seems to be a lot of fluff," John Billy said, wrapping up our discussion of religious dogma.

We were quiet for a while. Religious talk does that to a body. However, as soon as we crossed the Chattahoochee River, I asked John Billy why he left home to join the army.

"Well, it just built up over time. After the whacking he gave Deadeye Phagan, daddy was pretty cool-headed for some time. I think he realized he could have killed the boy. I mean, he would still beef at us boys and kick up a stink with the girls if they weren't working at every waking hour. There were occasional swats from him, but Mama took over the more weighty punishments. I think the last straw that broke the camel's back was like I was telling you before. He seemed most irritated when we stayed in bed too long, and too long was one second after he or Mama called."

"I had learned not to fiddle around in the mornings. There was no need to rankle him by dallying around. This one morning—this was long after Talmage and I had left school, and I think Paul was still finishing up at the grammar school, me and my daddy had a final blowout. Anyway, that morning he met me and Talmage on the stairs as we were coming down to do our morning chores before breakfast.

"'Before you boys tend the chickens and milk Bessie, you need to bring in some kindling for the woodstove so your mama can start breakfast. You should have done that last night while you were out there running around doing who knows what. You know she can't cook without kindling.' I could sense the peevishness in his voice.

"As we went through the kitchen toward the back of the house, I noticed that Mama had already started breakfast. She had enough kindling for breakfast, lunch, and supper. In as much as Daddy didn't have the opening to yell at us for getting up late, he decided to yell at us for not getting wood that we didn't even need.

"'Mama don't need no wood,' I said to him, but made sure I was on my way out the kitchen door before I said it.

"'Don't tell me what your mama needs, boy. If I tell you we need wood, you better get the wood without any lip about it,' he thundered back just as the screen door banged the jamb.

"When we were out of hearing distance of the kitchen, I vented to Talmage, 'Damn it Talmage. I ain't gonna take much more of him.'

"'Yeah, bbbut what are you gonna dddo?' he asked as he was buckling the second strap of his overalls.

"'I don't know,' I answered. 'I might just leave.'

"'Yeah, well, bbbefore you leave, we better hustle our bbbutts out to the woodpile. We gotta get some firewood for breakfast,' he said, laughing. "As we ambled our way to the woodpile, Talmage stopped suddenly and stuck his nose in the air like a hound sniffing for a buried soup bone. 'Holy mmmoly. I smell Mama's bbbiscuits. I'll be right back.'

"As Talmage ran back toward the house, I warned him, 'You better get your sorry ass over to that woodpile.'

"'Daddy's in the outhouse by now,' he yelled back. I knew he was right. That was another of his rituals that was timed to perfection. 'I'll be finished eating bbbiscuits before he gets dddone.'

"Talmage returned. His jaws, bleeding butter and strawberry jam, were the size of hog shanks.

"'You didn't get me one?' I asked him.

"'Mmmy hayans'—garbled Talmage, with no room for his tongue to move, 'wwwah full.'

"'I've got to get me a biscuit,' I said."

"'You ain't got tttime now bbbig brother. The old man ain't so ffffull of shit that it's gggonna take him all day in there.'

"'I'm going,' I said to Talmage, hoping he would talk me out of it. He made no effort. He sat on the woodpile waiting for the fireworks.

"'He's gonna bbbust your ass,' he warned.

"Exiting the outhouse and making his way toward the wood pile, Daddy spotted Talmage as he was wolfing the last morsel of jam and biscuit." "'Where is John Billy?' Daddy demanded of Talmage.

"Talmage stumbled for an explanation just as I came out the back-door with a biscuit in each hand and one crowding my gullet."

"Daddy's voice buckled my knees.'What are you doing, boy? Don't you know we don't eat around here until after we work? Do you think you are on relief?'

"'Well, Talmage got some bis—'

"Daddy interrupted me in mid explanation. 'I told you not to talk back to me! I'm gonna tear you up.'

"Daddy reached for a log from the woodpile. I had seen this before. 'You are not going to hit me with that. You nearly killed Deadeye Phagan. You are not going to kill me,' I said, while trying to hold back my tears.

"Daddy started toward me. I knew he had lost all self-control. I threw my two uneaten butter and jelly biscuits at him and then I ran. 'I hate you, you… son of a bitch,' I yelled back at him.

"Spewing tobacco juice, he yelled,'Boy, you can't talk to me like that! Come here and take your punishment! Come back here!'

"I stopped. My tears were washing away the butter and jam from my lips as I thought about going back. Then Daddy bent down and picked up three rocks. Fortunately, he was not the marksman that Talmage was. He missed me by inches. I heard Talmage tell him he needed to practice his rock throwing and offered to give him some pointers. He threw his last rock at Talmage, missing both Talmage and the woodpile.

"I ran and didn't stop until I hit the city limits of Tallapoosa.

"It was four and a half months before I saw Daddy again. I had not gone back home. Miss Estelle Ellerby had hired me on for room and board in return for helping her with her farm. Her husband, Cefus, had died the previous winter from kidney failure. Daddy and Talmage were in Tallapoosa to pick up feed. Talmage spotted me first."

"'Daddy, there is John Billy across the street,' I heard him say."

"Daddy stepped away from his Ford. He hesitantly approached me. I was determined to show no fear. I didn't run. In fact, I moved toward him. I felt protected in the open streets.

"'John Billy,' Daddy said, his voice cracking. 'John Billy, son, where have you been staying?'

"'I took a room with Miss Estelle Ellerby. She lets me work for my keep,' I said, while making sure not to lose my gaze into his eyes. He was looking at the ground.

"'Son,' Daddy said apologetically, 'I need you on the place. Talmage can't work. He never could.'

"I dropped my head, knowing this was the only apology I was going to get. I waited for Daddy to continue.

"'Son, I'll pay you'—he hesitated—'a dollar and a half a day.'

"'You promise not to hit me again?'

"'I won't hit you again,' he said. "I knew he meant it.

"'What about Talmage and Paul and the girls? No hitting them either?'

"'Agreed'

"Of course, we were all near grown, except for Paul, so that was an easy deal for him to make, but at least I got him to agree.

"With tears filling my eyes, I said, 'I'll see you in the morning.'

"I went back to the farm but promised myself that as soon as I turned eighteen, I would leave for good."

Chapter 13

Family Ties... and Binds

I had tears in my eyes, and I could see that John Billy had gotten a little misty eyed himself.

Once we passed the Chattahoochee River, it seemed that about every fifteen miles or so we would pass through a mirror of small towns. John Billy explained that these were all railroad towns and that Highway 78 ran right parallel along the tracks. Trains would stop for water and to drop off the mail and to pick up and drop passengers. Austell, Lithia Springs, Douglasville, Villa Rica, and Bremen were all rail-road stopping points before we reached Tallapoosa, the final stop before Alabama.

I had the jimmy-jammers the nearer we got to Tallapoosa. After the past eight hours, I felt as if I knew John Billy's family. Now all I needed was a face to match the personality.

Mr. Bailey was sitting on the porch, overseeing his family of field workers—Paul, Lazelle Post, and a skinny boy I took for Broomstick. They were all recognizable from John Billy's descriptions. Mr. Bailey took a misguided spit toward his brass spittoon as he stood to welcome us to his home. He and John Billy shared a cursory, yet not totally cold greeting.

From a distance, Mr. Bailey appeared taller than he actually was. His wiry body gave him the appearance of being taller than John Billy, but upon closer inspection they were both the same height. His shirt and trousers were rather baggy, so I assumed he had been fuller years back. John Billy's hair was beginning to thin on top. His pa's head was baby bare apart from a circle of pure white hair along the flanks. From looking at Mr. Bailey, I could tell that John Billy would be bareheaded in a few years. Mr. Bailey sported a flowing mustache that was stained walnut brown from years of chewing tobacco.

"Daddy, this is Mary. Mary, my daddy," John Billy said with very little enthusiasm.

"Mary, I am so happy to meet you," he said in a voice that seemed genuine. "My, you are a little one aren't you?" he continued.

"Mr. Bailey, I'm glad to meet you too. I have heard so much about you."

He smiled an "I'll bet you have" smile and said, "Well come on in and meet Miss Sarah."

John Billy went toward the field to see his sibling and the Posts as I followed Mr. Bailey into the house.

"Miss Sarah, look what John Billy brought home," he announced.

Miss Sarah came from the kitchen, drying her hands with a dish towel. She welcomed me with a warm, welcoming smile and little else.

"I love your home. It's so big. It's nothing like our house back on the island," I said, not knowing what else to say. It's like talking about the weather. It's always a good icebreaker. Just when I was about to comment on how Georgia was not as hot as Charleston, John Billy and Paul came barging in through the front door with our luggage.

"Y'all quit fooling around and take the suitcases up to Talmage and John Billy's old room," Miss Sarah instructed. "I'm going to show Mary around."

I could smell the recognizable aroma of collards boiling. It was unmistakable. The stink was a poor man's bouquet. Shadowing the collard ambience were the whiff and mystique of oak and hickory smoke that had permeated the walls after years of fireplace and woodstove use. Miss Sarah's kitchen was plain and functional but not something I could get used to. My focus was on the table in the center of the room as I visualized John Billy throwing a fork at Talmage and hiding under the table to avoid his pa's punches.

The living room was spacious but didn't appear to get much usage. I presumed that the family spent all sunlit hours working and moonlit hours sleeping. Leisure hours would be wanting for the Bailey family.

As Miss Sarah approached the stairs leading up to John Billy's room, I hesitated. Thoughts of Mr. Bailey striking the boys entered my head. I took a deep breath and followed her up the stairs. John Billy and Paul were wrestling on the floor.

"Boys, get up from there. Your daddy needs some help out at the barn before it gets too dark," she said very pleasantly. They were still tussling as they exited the room.

Miss Sarah was very agreeable and good tempered, but she had very little to say at first meeting. In fact, everyone in the house was remote to a fault except for John Billy's younger brother Paul. He talked to everyone, but none of them seemed to listen to anything he had to say. I listened, so he talked to me a lot. He was sixteen years old, about my age. He talked a lot about joining the navy. I suppose he had similar plans to those of all of his brothers and sisters—get out as soon as his age allowed.

Brother Talmage, I had been told by John Billy, had become a gad-about, drifting from one of the older brothers to another by hopping trains. He worked odd jobs when work could be found. When we arrived in Tallapoosa, he had an assignment with the Civil Conservation Corps in Villa Rica, Georgia, but it was understood that very soon he would be enlisting in the army. John Billy's twin sisters had also sprung loose, both marrying within weeks of each other. Iola had married Deadeye Phagan much to the chagrin of the entire Bailey family. I suppose joining the military was not an option for escaping home life for Iola, so Deadeye Phagan became her out.

Deadeye Phagan was in the pulpwood business with his father and spent all his waking hours cutting and hauling trees. Iola, like me, had not learned to drive a car, so she was not able to greet us when we arrived in Tallapoosa but she had left word for us to come by her house for supper and to spend the night after we got settled at John Billy's parents.

It didn't take me long to discover that life in Tallapoosa, Georgia was a lot different from life on Sullivan's Island. I thought Miss Sarah was going to lose her breath when I asked her where the bathroom was.

"It's in the barn," she told me after her laughter died.

"In the barn?"

"Well, it isn't exactly in the barn," she said. "It is the barn. Come, I'll show you."

Miss Sarah wasn't lying. She said I could use the bathroom anywhere I wanted as long as the cow or two mules didn't object.

"But where is the toilet?" I asked, thinking to myself that Tallapoosa wasn't much on privacy.

"We don't got no toilet," she explained. "The men use the outhouse, but that old thing is crumbling. You have to go clean into town to find a sit-down toilet.

"Out here in the barn you got two choices. You can just squat, but that puts you too close to the ground, and as hard as this red dirt is it will just splatter all over you. Or here is what I do. You can stick your legs through this here stall rail and hold on to the top rail for balance. It's a bit cumbersome, but at least it keeps you off the ground so you don't sprinkle yourself. At night, you can use the piss pot that's under your bed, but you will have to empty it in the morning."

Miss Sarah demonstrated her stall-sitting skill, but I was afraid I wouldn't be able to keep my balance and take care of business at the same time. I took my chances on splattering my bottom on the hard, red-clay floor of the barn. As it turned out, there was no way to avoid the splashing. If I squatted low, I splashed my bottom. If I squatted high, I splashed my ankles. All the while as I was trying to fashion my squat, Miss Sarah kept laughing at me.

"You look like Mr. Bailey's car jack, but don't worry—you will get the hang of it."

Miss Sarah told me that she had not laughed like that since she was a little girl. I could see why she would say that too. Mr. Bailey didn't seem to care much for giggles. On occasion, he would smile at something Paul did or said, but he yelled at him more than he smiled at him.

During our two weeks in Tallapoosa, I pressed Miss Sarah to tell me about her history—where she was born, how she grew up, how she met Mr. Bailey.

She grew up in Gwinnett County, near the Loganville city line in a community called Bay Creek. I told her we had passed through there, but had not stopped. Her great-grandfather had settled there and built up quite a business of a general store, grist mill, and buggy shop which he and his four sons ran. Her grandfather had attended a military school in Marietta, Georgia, and became a schoolteacher. When the Civil War broke out, he helped organize a company in Gwinnett County and headed off to Virginia. He fought with Robert E. Lee,

Stonewall Jackson, and A. P. Hill. He rose to the rank of major by the war's end. All three of his brothers either died of the smallpox or were killed. After the war, he came home and became the postmaster of Bay Creek and eventually became a state representative from the area. I could tell she was very proud of her great-grandfather. After the war, most of his kin moved to Texas, but he stayed in Gwinnett and made the most of things by farming. Most of that part of Georgia was devastated from Sherman's March. Her father continued to farm and was very active in the Farmer's Alliance, but life was a struggle for many years after the war.

She grew up with a loving father and grandfather, both of whom doted on her and her sister. Her prospects for marriage were slim until Mr. Bailey came riding by in his fancy wagon. She explained, as had John Billy, that at her mother's urging, she had allowed herself to be courted by Mr. Bailey, thinking he was a man of means. She knew he had lost a wife and had three boys and the baby twin girls, but he was an optional prospect to a life as an old maid.

Apparently, plans were brewing for me and John Billy to live with his parents, help them with the farm, and eventually assume ownership of the farm. When John Billy broached the subject to me, I didn't say much, but I knew from the first that that would never work. John Billy and his pa rarely said a word to each other, and while we were there, John Billy and Paul did all the work while Mr. Bailey supervised from his rocker on the front porch.

Sometime during our second week in Tallapoosa, I think John Billy had had enough of his pa bossing him around, so he suggested that we take up Iola on her offer for supper and an over night stay. She and Deadeye lived north of Tallapoosa, a short drive from the Bailey farm. We had not seen Iola yet, but I think our visit was more to get out from under the command of Mr. Bailey than to visit with Iola and Deadeye.

On the drive over, John Billy reminded me that Deadeye was no more than white trash and that he was very disappointed with his sister for marrying him. He said all the Phagans were as sorry as the day was long, and he couldn't understand why his pa would allow the marriage in the first place. But I knew why Iola had married Deadeye. She wanted to escape her situation, just as I had a need to escape my own, so she married the first man to ask for her hand.

Iola was only a few years older than John Billy, but her eyes had the look of age. She looked worn out, and I found out why when Deadeye Phagan came home in his pulp wood truck. While her eyes looked distant and tired, his eyes had the look of evil—one with the drooping lid and the other in a frozen stare. His lips were pinched together and turned down at the corners, giving him a permanent scowl. He was in need of a haircut and shave, but most of all he needed a bath. He smelled as bad as he looked.

"You got supper ready?" he said to Iola without even acknowledging John Billy or me.

"No," she said. "John Billy came home from the army, and he got married. We've been visiting."

"I'm going to go over to Daddy's for supper. I'll be back later," he said, again without giving John Billy or me the time of day.

"They are going to spend the night with us tonight, Junior," Iola yelled to Deadeye just as he got back in his pulpwood truck to drive over to his pa's.

"We'll go back to Daddy's if you think we should," John Billy told Iola.

"No, please stay," she said, almost pleading. "I haven't talked to anyone out here in almost four months."

We talked nonstop for hours. The only time we broke from conversation was when she set the table for supper. I helped her spoon the collards and butter the corn bread while she carved the chicken. I could tell that there was a special bond between Iola and John Billy. Her face lit up with his every word, and I could tell she was the most kind-hearted of souls, wanting to please us with every impassioned endeavor, be it feeding us or preparing our pallet on the floor.

Iola only had one bedroom in her house, so she fixed a pallet of quilts for us on the living room floor. We weren't in bed ten minutes when we heard Deadeye's pulp wood truck pull up into the yard. It sounded as if he were tearing out the gears until he finally cut off the motor.

As soon as Deadeye stepped onto the porch, he screamed out to Iola, "Has your damned company gone yet?"

"He's drunk," Iola whispered from her bedroom. "He always gets drunk when he visits with his daddy. His daddy is a bootlegger."

Iola got out of bed to help Deadeye from the porch to their bed. There was a lot of commotion in their bedroom, but we couldn't make out what they were saying with Iola whispering lower than when she called out to us about him being drunk and Deadeye slurring his words.

"I'm scared," I exhaled in a whisper to John Billy.

"Don't worry. He's drunk. He will pass out as soon as he hits the bed. We will leave early in the morning, before he gets up."

Through the open door, we could make out the shadowy outlines of Iola and Deadeye as she struggled with him, trying to get him into bed.

"I want my damned supper ready when I get home, and I don't care who the hell is visiting," we heard him say, well above the previous whisper.

"Hush, Junior. John Billy and Mary are in the living room trying to sleep. Now come on, get in bed," she said with more than a whisper but still not at his volume.

"I don't care if they are sleeping in our bed. This is my house. I'll say what-ever the hell I please and to whoever I please. Now get out of my way," he screamed as he slapped her backhanded across the face. We heard her hit the bed.

John Billy was off the floor before I could even think about stopping him, and I don't think I could have stopped him even if I tried. His fist caught Deadeye in the back of the head, knocking him side straddle on the bed right beside Iola, who was by this time, trying to get up.

I was up but couldn't see well. The room was dim, especially near the bed, with the only light coming from an oil lamp on the dresser and the faint glow of an overcast moon, but I could hear Deadeye's cries with each smack from John Billy's knuckled fist. While the beating continued, I crawled over to Iola, who was now on the floor beside the dresser. We both pleaded for John Billy to stop his unmerciful thrashing of Deadeye for fear that he was going to kill him in the blackness of their bedroom. When Deadeye quit screaming, John Billy stopped pounding.

"Let's get some sleep," John Billy finally said after regaining his breathing. "Deadeye can sleep this one off."

"Do you think he is OK?" I asked.

"Well, if he ain't, the world hasn't lost much," John Billy said, as he made his way back to our pallet.

"That's for sure," said Iola, who was still sitting beside me on the floor. "If y'all don't mind, I think I'll make me a pallet besides y'all's."

Chapter 14

Bees and Flies and Snakes and Rats—Oh My

The next morning Iola and John Billy and I were up early. Deadeye didn't stir at all. We could tell that he was going to be all right because he was snoring. I didn't want to look at him, but I was drawn like a moth to a flame to take a gander at him. He was pretty bloody and swollen. I thought to myself that a few stitches and a bath would fix him right up.

John Billy and I didn't stay for breakfast. I didn't want to be around when Deadeye stirred for fear that John Billy would kill him if he tried to avenge his shellacking.

Iola didn't seem upset over the episode. She said that Junior got that way when he drank, but he wasn't so bad when he was sober.

"You don't have to stay with him. You are welcome to come stay with us in Charleston," John Billy told her.

"Well, I'm certainly not going to go back home and live with Daddy. I'd rather take my chances with Junior. Besides, I'm gonna have a baby," she replied.

"Iola, if you are going to have a baby, he shouldn't be hitting you like that. If I had known that, I would have killed him last night. He has no business hitting you while you are pregnant. You let me know if he ever hits you again. Now you look here—me and Mary ain't going to be here much longer, so if you need a place to stay, you are always welcome to come stay with us," John Billy told her, almost pleading.

On the way back to his ma's and pa's I asked John Billy what he meant by saying we weren't going to be with his ma and pa much longer.

"I thought you were laying plans to take over the farm from your pa someday?" I asked him.

"I'm not sure it's going to work out. Don't you want to go back to Charleston?" he asked.

"I don't want to go back unless you do, but I want you to make sure yourself. On the way here, you talked about having a farm of your own. If we go back to Charleston, you won't get to farm unless you can grow rice or sand fleas. You will probably regret it the rest of your life," I reasoned, with little enthusiasm.

"Well, we are in no big hurry. We have plenty of time to decide," he said. "Employment is on the upswing in Charleston. There are government jobs. I can drive most any large vehicle. The army taught me that."

As things shook out, we didn't have as much time as we thought. John Billy and his pa were still not communicating, and I was still working on my potty training technique in the barn stalls. It appeared that we were settling into the routine of farm life in Tallapoosa, Georgia. It was a week after John Billy had battered Deadeye Phagan to a pulpy mess that I came to realize that I didn't belong in Tallapoosa, Georgia.

I just never could adjust fully to that lifestyle in the Bailey home. No one talked except Paul. The trek to the barn every time I had to use the toilet became so repulsive that I almost quit going. The thought of sweet Iola living alone with that sadistic Deadeye Phagan kept me in constant tears. The flies were unmerciful, no thanks to the unscreened windows. There were honeybees in the walls of the attic that I expected would swarm on me in the middle of the night. It was all too much for me. And when I found a black snake in my bed, I knew it was time to return to the civilized world of Charleston.

The snake meant no harm. In fact, Paul knew it by name because it usually stayed in the barn, where it ate rats and mice. Paul called the snake Lester Joseph Gillis, which, I learned, was Baby Face Nelson's birth name. John Billy told me it likely came inside because of the weather changing, but I am not sure even to this day that Paul and John Billy didn't place it there for sport. John Billy assured me it was helpful in keeping the rodents at bay. I didn't believe him, even after I saw Paul pick it up and take it back to the barn.

"I want to go home," I cried that night. "I can't take another day here. There are bees and flies and snakes and rats everywhere, and no one seems to take notice, and if they did they wouldn't talk about it. And you, you have to beat up your brother-in-law for beating up your sister, and I can't use the toilet anymore. This place is driving me loco, and I want to go home."

John Billy promised me we would leave, and we did, just one month after we had arrived in Tallapoosa. Miss Sarah was sad to see us go. I was the only female company she had had since Iola and Viola had left home. I'm not sure what Mr. Bailey felt about us leaving or anything else for that matter. Paul was even more saddened to see us leave because he was now left alone to hammer it out with his pa. Of course, he reminded us that he was joining the navy as soon as he could.

I too was saddened to leave them all behind, but they left my thoughts as soon as I crossed the Cooper River Bridge and was as firmly planted on Sullivan's Island as one of the low country palmettos.

SULLIVAN'S ISLAND, SOUTH CAROLINA

Chapter 15

Motherhood

John Billy and I had but little choice than to move in with my ma and pa and Sis in Uncle Frank's island house. Pa had long ago finished his trade deal with Uncle Frank — rent for a paint job and repairs. He was now paying cash for rent. Our moving in with them helped with the rent. Pa said he was moving out of Uncle Frank's place as soon as he got on his feet again. He never got on his feet again, so he and Ma lived with us for the rest of their lives.

It was peculiar how things had changed on the island in the few short weeks we were in Tallapoosa. Sis was seeing regularly a military man from Illinois who was stationed in Charleston. He had the very discomfiting name of Morris Rape. Ma was tending to a newborn baby when we returned. Her account was that it had been abandoned by its young mother and she took it in because she didn't want it to end up in the orphanage like me and Sis. However, island whispers, according to Sis, were that the baby actually belonged to my pa from a misbegotten fling with Annamarie Messina, the island punch. Ma, in her irreproachable goodness, could not suffer to see a child or animal in harm's way.

My ma was notorious for her kind heart and generosity. I remember once, just before we went into the orphanage when she and Sis and I were walking along East Bay Street, and we came upon a woman lying naked on the steps of a warehouse. A policeman was standing there but seemed addled as to what to do with her. My ma lit into him like a hound on a rabbit. "Young man," she said. "Have you no decency? That could be somebody's sister. Take off your jacket and cover that young lady. Can't you see she is on hard times just like the rest of us?"

"I was trying to get her up so I could take her down to the station," he started before Ma abruptly interrupted him.

"You will do no such thing. That girl needs medical attention. We will take her over to Roper. You help me get her into your car."

Turning to me and Sis, she said, "Girls, y'all go on home now. Tell your pa I'll be home directly. Me and this young gentleman are going to the hospital."

That was Ma's nature. She, without showing any outward fury, possessed an inner rage when it came to the destitute. Her heart and spirit guided her emotions toward generosity. She was the most charitable person I had ever known.

My pa, notwithstanding his crutches, was an attractive man. He had the gift of gab and was flirtatious. Sis and I called it the gift of blab, but it did attract some women. I guess that is how he charmed my ma. His charm must have worked on Annamarie Messina as well—that and his bath tub wine.

The baby was called Angelina. I was never clear on who christened the child with that name, but I suspect Annamarie Messina had leverage in the selection. Sis and I knew Ma was not up to mothering a newborn. Try as we might, we could not get Ma to see the error in her act of kindness. The orphanage option was definitely out, but our friend and neighbor, Gladys Snowden, offered to take the child in. Gladys took in stray children the way the dog catcher took in stray mongrels. And there were plenty of both to choose from during the Depression.

After months of begging and pleading from Sis and me and Pa, Ma agreed to allow Angelina to move on to Gladys's. But I think it was John Billy's hint that Ma would soon enough be a grandmother that pushed her over to giving up Angelina. Ma knew Gladys well, and she knew Gladys had a long history of fostering unwanted guttersnipe. Ma's only reservation was Mr. Snowden. Freddy Snowden was a plumber and a boozehound—a hard worker when sober and the devil when crocked. Ma always said, "Freddy Snowden is up to no good."

Having the baby Angelina around for a while was a good thing for me. I took to changing, feeding, and dressing her and tending to her squalls. She squalled like no other. While I was being schooled in the fine art of infant care, John Billy found the foundling fractious. "That baby ain't right. She just ain't right," he would say, whenever she erupted onto one of her frenzies.

John Billy very quickly was able to get a WPA job doing construction work at the Citadel. Back around when I was born, the academy had moved from its downtown location to the west side of Charleston. That and the winding down of the Depression made for lots of construction job opportunities.

I was indeed pregnant, and nine months after returning from Tallapoosa, I gave birth to our first boy. So there we were—Ma and Pa, John Billy and me and Johnny, and Sis. The island house was scarcely big enough for Ma and Pa and John Billy and me. Ma and Pa had a room, and me and John Billy had a room. Sis slept on the sofa bed in the living room, while Johnny slept in the sock drawer of our chest-of-drawers.

A year and two months later, John Billy and I had our second boy, Joseph, named after my pa. Joseph inherited Johnny's sock drawer, and Johnny moved over to the sofa bed with Sis.

Sis was envious, if not jealous, of my marriage and baby. She and Morris Rape announced their marriage and pregnancy not long after the birth of Joseph, our second son. Morris Rape then moved in with us and into Sis's sofa bed. Johnny then pitched between our bedroom and Ma and Pa's.

Sis gave birth to Hedy, who was named after the up and coming Hollywood actress, Hedy Lamarr. The mathematical mystery of who slept where was resolved prior to the birth of Hedy when Morris Rape was shipped to an air station in Texas. It seemed that airplane mechanics were in demand and he was assigned to Lackland's army air corp in San Antonio.

When the Japanese attacked Pearl Harbor in December, John Billy wanted to re-enlist in the army. Paul had joined the navy and Talmage, by this time, was already serving in the army. In fact, he had been at Schofield since June of 1940. As luck would have it, he and a friend were returning to housing after a weekend pass presented them with a few nights on the town. The two of them and the cab driver found refuge under a bridge until the attack was over. His training intensified, and his unit was placed into service in the Pacific Islands for the war's duration. Paul also found his way eventually to the Pacific. By August of 1942, both brothers were part of the Pacific operations. Talmage was with the army infantry in a chemical company. This meant that he operated a flamethrower. Paul, on the other hand, was a ship's cook on a destroyer.

I convinced John Billy that he needed to stay home with me. He had served his time and duty in Panama, and besides, we had two boys and a third child on the way. I don't know if my pleading convinced him to stay home or the fact that he was recently hired on as a bus driver for the city of Charleston. In any event, he did not re-enlist. With his new job driving from Mount Pleasant to Charleston, John Billy realized he was better off on Sullivan's Island than fighting the heat and bugs on some Japanese island or driving a tank in North Africa.

Chapter 16

Yo' Daddy Is Lucifer; War Is Hell

After our little girl Barbara was born, John Billy determined that I needed help with my growing brood and that perhaps more help was needed with my ma and pa, as their health was beginning to wane. I told him that I was fine. I really didn't need the extra help. Sis helped a little, and Ma was a comfort with the two boys. But John Billy was determined and wasn't much for being dissuaded once his mind was made up. Besides, he was making good money, what with the war going on. He decided to hire a colored lady three days a week to help with the cleaning and ironing.

The first woman he hired was Ethel Coot. Ethel stayed with us only two weeks. My pa ran her off. He hated the colored and didn't want Ethel in our house or around his grandchildren. Accordingly, he made her life dreadfully abhorrent.

"Yo' pappy is the devil," she told me at the end of her first day on the job.

"What are you talking about, Ethel?" I asked her.

"That white man scares me. He breathes the fire of Lucifer."

"Don't you pay any attention to him," I told her. "I've lived with him for over twenty-two years. He won't hurt you."

I kept my eye on my pa for the next couple of days when Ethel was working. He didn't seem to be bothering her, but she stayed clear of him when she worked, even to the point of going out the front door and walking around the house to the backyard to gather the clothes from the line just to avoid going through his bedroom.

A few days before Ethel quit working for us I had to go to Mr. Rosetti's market, which meant I had to leave Ethel alone with my pa for an hour or so.

I said to her, "Ethel, I have to go to the market for some things for supper. I'll be back in a while."

She protested, "Oh no, Miss Mary Margaret. Don't leave me alone here with that old white man. He'll cut my heart out. He told me he would. Let me go to Mr. Rosetti's for yo' groceries."

"Ethel, quit being so silly. My pa won't hurt you. You just stay here in the kitchen and do your ironing. I'll tell my Pa to leave you alone. Remember, he's crippled. He could never catch you," I said to her, trying to calm her nerves.

"Yeh, dat's a sign he was born of the devil," she argued.

"He wasn't born that way," I countered, but I quickly realized that there was no reasoning with her about my pa's kinship with the devil.

After telling Pa to leave Ethel alone while I was at Rosetti's, I left for the market. No sooner was I off the front porch and in the yard than I heard my pa call from his bedroom.

"Coooooot. Coooooot. Ethel Coooooot"

"Mr. Jakey, you leave me alone," she begged. "I got this hot iron in here."

I made my way back to the porch but didn't go into the house. Something inside me wanted to watch this play out.

"Ethel Coot, you come here, damn it. I need you to see about my leg, and bring that iron with you," Pa said, with a voice of desperation.

"Mr. Jakey, Miss Mary Margaret told me to stay in the kitchen, and she told you to stay in yo' bedroom. Now, you leave me alone, now."

"Ethel Coot, I need you to see about my leg. It's hurting me real bad. I won't bother you. I promise. I just need you to take a look at my leg," Pa said, rather pleadingly. But then with a change of tongue, he yelled, "Damn it. Get in here."

Scared out of her wits, Ethel replied, "OK, Mr. Jakey, but if you hurt me I'll scorch you with this iron."

Through the screen door, I watched Ethel inch her way from the kitchen toward Pa's bedroom. She held the iron at arm's length, straining her neck to peek over it in anticipation that Pa would jump out at her at any moment. Little did she know that I had taken Pa's crutches from the bedroom just before I left for the market.

"Ethel Coot, come over here."

Ethel snailed her way closer to Pa's bed.

"Ethel Coot," Pa said to her when she was close enough to his bed to see he was under his covers. "Whenever my leg gets to hurting this bad, I get someone to iron it for me to get the wrinkles out."

With that said, he belted back the covers to expose to Ethel his polio-stricken leg. Ethel bolted out of my pa's bedroom, down the hallway, and out the front door past me, screaming, "Satan's tail! I done seen the tail of the devil."

She didn't stop running until she reached the edge of the hot-tar-and-graveled street. She held up the iron as a crucifix to ward off the evils coming from the hainted house on Station 26 1/2.

"Satan begone! Satan begone! In the name of Jesus on the cross, have mercy on my wicked soul, and take Satan from Miss Mary Margaret's home," she prayed, attempting to exorcise the darkness from my home.

"Ethel, Satan is not in my home," I said to her, trying to alleviate her obvious dread. "Now you bring that iron back here and finish up your work. My pa is just trying to get your goat, and you are letting him. Don't pay him no mind."

"I can't go back in that house. It's been possessed by the devil hisself. I seen him in there. No, ma'am. Ethel Coot ain't gone be no part of that."

I knew there was no talking sense to her. I sent her home for the remainder of the day.

"You go on home and settle down. You can come back on Friday to finish up the ironing," I told her.

"No, ma'am. I can't go back in the house. The devil will take me home."

I knew she would be back on Friday. Friday was her payday.

Pa was waiting at the kitchen table when Ethel Coot came into work on Friday. She appeared to have resolved her issues with our bedeviled house; however, she was wearing around her neck a freshly amputated rabbit's foot and a wreath of woven garlic bulbs and stems. She had made the sign of the cross on her forehead from the char of a burned match head. She was prepared.

I was tending Barbara when she came in. She hesitated when she saw that Pa was sitting in the kitchen, but her false sense of security allowed her to bravely enter. I spoke, but Pa said nothing to Ethel. He couldn't. When he saw her coming up the front steps, he filled his bottom lip with kerosene. As she entered, he lit a match, and just as she was greeting me, he spit the kerosene toward the lighted match, which he held at arms length from his face. A ball of fire greeted Ethel, who fell flat back on the kitchen linoleum.

"That girl is as crazy as a coot," he said, laughing at his little play on words.

Ethel quit working for us on that Friday, but John Billy had already found a replacement because he knew Ethel wasn't going to be with us much longer. The new help was an older lady from Mount Pleasant. Her name was Margaret. We called her Black Margaret so that no one would confuse her with me. She would ride in with John Billy on the ten o'clock bus on his return trip from his morning route to Charleston, and she would ride back with him on his afternoon route back to the peninsula.

From day one Black Margaret was methodical with her cleaning. She began in my ma's and pa's room. My ma was an early riser and was already feeding her chickens and talking to them and to herself when Black Margaret came to work on her first day. Pa slept late and was still in bed when Black Margaret entered his bedroom to change the bed-sheets.

"Mr. Jakey, you are going to have to get out of bed before I get here because I have work to do, and I ain't got no time to mess with you and your foolishness in the mornings. Now if you will kindly get up, I will change your bed linen," she insisted.

"Who the hell are you to demand that I get out of my own bed?"

"I'm Black Margaret, and I work for Mr. John Billy. So if you will kindly get out of that bed, I will do my work," she said to Pa as she handed him his crutch.

Pa immediately went for his kerosine and matches. The ball of flame left no bearing on Black Margaret.

"Old man," she said to him. "If you burn this house down, where do you think these babies gonna sleep?"

"Well, hell's bells," he stuttered. "How should I know?"

"Das right. You don't know. You don't know nothing. So if you will quit messing with me, I'll make up this bed and go about my business," she said to Pa, almost ignoring him as she continued to pull off the old sheets right from under him.

"Well, I'll be damned, if that don't beat all," my pa said, as he quickly got out of harms way.

Black Margaret took an immediate liking to my ma, and my ma to her. They were constant companions whenever Black Margaret had a free moment from her daily duties. At lunch or in the afternoons before John Billy's bus was ready to return her to Mount Pleasant, they took walks along the beach. My ma would talk to Black Margaret some of the time and to herself the rest of the time. Black Margaret always knew to whom she was speaking.

"Black Margaret is the best friend I ever had," Ma would say to my pa. "She don't try to tell me what to do like you do, and my sisters do, and everybody else."

Ma and Black Margaret remained the best of friends until we laid Ma to rest in the Saint Lawrence Cemetery in the fall of 1944. She was playing with Johnny on her bed when she lay back and said to Johnny, "Go fetch your ma. I'm too tired."

Shortly after Ma passed, the Selective Service decided it might need John Billy's services after all. Attrition had diminished the number of fighting soldiers by the end of 1944, so, consequently, there was a push to take a look at those young men who had previous experience soldiering.

John Billy got his call. He explained to the draft board that he had four children. Yes, we had a second girl, Sarah, born just months before Ma's passing. He also explained that he had a crippled father-in-law and a mother-in-law who had just passed. Plus, he had two brothers who were already fighting in the Pacific. The draft board, with the compassion of a Carolina sand shark, offered John Billy an out to being re-enlisted in the army. He was told that if he took an essential war-industry job at the navy yard, they wouldn't draft him. John Billy told the board that he enjoyed driving the bus for the City of Charleston and that he would not work at the navy yard.

John Billy and the draft board bandied about for a few months as to where he would work until the board got tired of the wrangling and called him to active service. John Billy was a stubborn man. He felt that he had served his country in Panama and his personal circumstances should allow him the deferment from having to serve a second tour. The draft board disagreed and by March he was sent off to Fort Knox, Kentucky, for seventeen weeks of training at the Armored Replacement Training Center for a repeat of instruction in the use of the more modern tanks that had been developed during the war.

At this point John Billy was ready to be deployed. He had resigned himself to the fact that he was needed when he received word that his brother Talmage had been taken captive by the Japs and was a prisoner of war on some island in the Pacific.

John Billy made it as far as California to be shipped out to the Pacific, but his deployment was cut short when the Americans bombed the Japanese cities of Nagasaki and Hiroshima.

We never heard directly from Talmage until the war was over. He went back home to his ma and pa in Tallapoosa. His ma, Miss Sarah, wrote to us about what Talmage had suffered. As a member of the chemical company, he was assigned to support the marines as they went island to island sweeping out the Japanese from their entrenchments. He was there for the liberation of the Marshall Islands and some of the places I remember reading about—Palau, Peleliu, and Ryukyu—names I can't pronounce.

Talmage was awarded the Bronze Star, the Philippine Liberation Ribbon with two Bronze Stars and the Asiatic Pacific Theater Ribbon with four Bronze Stars. He was almost killed when he attempted to escape his prisoner-of-war confinement. Talmage, as a flamethrower, had to burn men alive who were hidden away in spider holes or underground retreats. In her letters Miss Sarah said that Talmage had lost forty-seven pounds, but had gained most of it back since he had been eating her home cooking. She also told us that Talmage had changed. "He's not the same boy that left Tallapoosa seven years ago," she said in every letter she sent.

We found out soon enough how much Talmage had changed. Though I had never met him, I felt as if I knew Talmage well enough from the stories John Billy had told me about their growing up in Georgia. Talmage came to visit us in Charleston just after Christmas in 1946. He was no longer the boy John Billy had described.

His visit came at an inopportune time for me. I was eight months pregnant with my fifth child, and the other four had been sick off and on all winter. I was exhausted but welcomed him just the same.

Talmage was one of the most handsome men I had ever met. He was a small man but powerfully built, with an athletic jaw. He had deep-set blue eyes, and it was those eyes that gave away that he was not at peace with himself.

Talmage requested that he be allowed to sleep on a pallet on the floor, not because we didn't have enough beds but because he had not adjusted to sleeping in a bed yet. It was rare over the war's duration that he had cottoned to the comforts of a bed. I made him a pallet in the hallway of our quite crowded house.

On his first night with us Talmage's screams had us all barreling out of bed. John Billy, with blistering speed, rushed out to the hallway to awaken Talmage from God knows what nightmarish horror he was reliving. Miss Sarah had warned us about the screams, but we were ill prepared for them. Talmage tearfully apologized but said that he could make no promises that the nightmares would not continue. He explained that he had been having them since his return to the States. Most often he did not even remember the dream. He just awakened to find himself in a sweat of panic and dread. John Billy and I assured him that we understood, but we had no empathy for what he had gone through. If truth be known, his nightmares and screams held me in a constant state of jitters.

Talmage's screams continued like clockwork, as did the tears and apologies. Talmage was a troubled man, and this was never more evident than when he killed the children's new puppy.

We had acquired the puppy from a regular rider on John Billy's bus route, which, by the way, he had resumed after the war. Talmage had shown a fondness for the puppy. In fact, the puppy had taken to sleeping with Talmage on his pallet at night. In some ways, it had actually seemed to ease Talmage's nighttime agitation.

On the day Talmage killed the puppy, Johnny was home from school with the croup. He was feeding the puppy on our porch as he watched Joseph head off for school. Talmage came out on the porch and asked Johnny if he could hold the puppy.

"Sure, Uncle Talmage," I heard Johnny say, willingly handing the dog to its bunkmate.

Talmage very calmly held the dog upside down by its four legs and dropped it from the porch. Johnny's screams were near as loud as the puppy's, and they both brought me out to the porch in a flash of a second. I rushed to the puppy, along with Johnny, but its yelps had died by the time we got to it.

"Uncle Talmage killed my puppy," Johnny said, barely able to get the words out.

I looked up at Talmage, who was still standing on the porch where he had dropped the puppy. His eyes were glazed. I asked, "Talmage, why did you do that?"

Very coldly he replied, "He wasn't any good to anybody. He is just a black dog."

Talmage returned to Georgia shortly after the puppy's killing. Little did I know that he would be back in a few weeks.

Death-and-Life Situation

Johnny, my oldest, was a sickly child. He seemed to attract every child-hood bug that ran aground on Sullivan's Island. He missed most of his second year in school with a bout of the yellow jaundice. He had to repeat the grade, which placed him and Joseph in the same class the following year. He had to spend most of Thanksgiving and Christmas of 1946 in bed with the croup, and by the end of January he had con-tracted the measles. I expected that on any day one of the other children would come down with the croup or the measles or both.

Barbara was my healthiest child. She had not been sick a day in her life. Even as a wee baby, she seemed to avoid the petty ailments that the rest of my children seemed to attract. I don't even remember her having a diaper rash.

Barbara was as near a perfect child as any parent could want. She was her daddy's girl. No matter what she was doing, when her Daddy came home from his bus route, she would stop and go to him with hugs and kisses. They would walk hand in hand from the street corner to the front steps. John Billy would sit down on the steps and place Barbara on his lap and have her tell him about her day. At the supper table, Barbara had to sit by her daddy. Neither Johnny nor Joseph nor Sarah was jealous of her or of the bond she had with her daddy. They loved her as much as John Billy and I loved her.

My pa too had a special place in his heart for Barbara. He was forever saying to me, or to John Billy, or to Black Margaret, or to anyone else who would listen to him, "That baby is an angel. God won't share her with us for long. He will need her in heaven." I guess he was right.

As much as I hated to, I kept Johnny home from school. Sarah had a mild cough. Barbara, a year away from starting first grade, was without a cough or an eruption of red marks. So here I was, nine months pregnant, ready to birth my fifth child at any time, and home alone, except for my crippled pa and Black Margaret.

The day Barbara left us was like most any other on the island—full of life's routines. John Billy had his usual breakfast of two fried eggs, grits, ham, and home made biscuits with butter and syrup with a cup of black coffee. My pa had been up for breakfast, but he had returned back to his bed since Black Margaret had not yet arrived and wasn't there to pester him.

"I don't know why Black Margaret can't leave me the hell alone. She could clean my room last if she only would, but hell no, she has to come in here and disturb me first thing," he would say.

After my pa went back to sleep, I checked in on Johnny and gave him a little breakfast though he didn't feel much like eating. Barbara and Sarah asked if they could go out and play in the yard. I told them to play on the porch. I didn't want Sarah running around in the yard with her cough, but it was a rather warm day for January, so I thought the sun might do Sarah some good.

The sound of the Puckett Ice Company delivery truck caused me to look up from my coffee. Though I was used to the sound of the delivery truck on the days it came to dispense block ice for our icebox, the sound of the truck was louder than usual. From the kitchen window I could see down the tar-and-graveled road that the truck had stopped to deliver two blocks of ice to Gladys Snowden's. When the truck's engine shut off, I could hear Barbara and Sarah singing "Happy Birthday" to their most recent Christmas doll baby. Before the girls could finish with "and many more," the truck engine again drowned them out as it approached our house on Station 26 1/2.

Wilbur Ivey had been driving for Mr. Puckett for at least two years. He was a nice young man and very considerate. He always delivered to the back door, even though it meant he had to walk the extra distance for his delivery.

"Wilbur, your truck seems to be extra loud today," I said to him as I opened the back screen door for him to enter.

"Yes, ma'am," he said to me. "I think the clutch is slipping, and the exhaust muffler has a hole in it. I'm going to tell Mr. Puckett about it when we get back to Charleston."

"Looks like Mr. Puckett has hired you some help," I said to Wilbur as I looked out the door toward the ice truck parked in the yard. There was a colored boy sitting in the cab of the truck who looked to be in his late teens.

"Yes, ma'am. That's Flash. He's kinda slow, but I think he will be able to help me once I teach him to do deliveries and he learns how to talk to white people. Once I do that, he can make the deliveries and I can drive the truck. We will be able to work much faster that way," Wilbur explained.

As Wilbur was explaining to me about Flash and his plans for speeding up the delivery process, we made our way to the icebox. As I opened the door of the ice-box for Wilbur to place the ice in the box, I heard the roar of the engine of Mr. Puckett's ice truck.

"Flash must be turning the truck around," Wilbur said, more to himself than to me.

"Does Mr. Puckett allow him to drive the truck?" I asked Wilbur.

"No, ma'am. He ain't supposed to be—" He didn't finish.

"Mama, that truck just ran over Barbara." It was Johnny calling out from the living room.

"What? What did you say? I can't hear you for that truck," I called back. But I knew what he had said the minute Wilbur Ivey dropped his ice tongs on the kitchen floor and the second I heard Sarah's screams.

Wilbur Ivey instinctively ran out the back door, leaving me in the kitchen, and it wasn't until Johnny's tugs on my maternity blouse that I sprinted down the hall and out to the front porch.

Black Margaret had arrived earlier and was rousting my pa from his bed when she heard Johnny's call to me. She reached Barbara before I could negotiate the steps of the porch and was muffling Sarah's screams in her huge black breast. Wilbur Ivey, just as I leaped and fell down the steps, was flinging Flash from the cab of the truck. When I reached Barbara, she was motionless. I tried to pick her up in my arms, but her head was lodged between the two paired back wheels of the ice truck.

"Wilbur! Help! Help me!" I screamed.

Wilbur killed the truck engine and leapt from the cab of the truck. He tried to lift the truck from Barbara's head but was only able to move the bed. The wheels would not budge. Black Margaret released Sarah, who again began to wail uncontrollably, to help Wilbur lift the truck from my baby's head. My pa, with the help of Johnny and a single crutch, made his way to the rear of the truck. So there we were—a crippled old man, a house cleaner, a sick young boy, the ice truck driver, and me, a full-term pregnant woman, all trying to lift a half-loaded ice truck from Barbara.

"Flash!" I cried out to the obviously dim-witted colored boy who was still in the freeze tag position on the ground where Wilbur had thrown him. "Help us! You have killed my baby. Now help us save her."

Flash didn't move until my pa's cane and Black Margaret's foot caught him broadside at the same moment. He bolted up to his feet and immediately maneuvered his shoulders under the truck, nearest the wheels that had Barbara's head pinned to the sandy yard.

With Flash helping the others, I was able to slide the limp body from under the wheel of the truck. Barbara was dead. Although I couldn't see from the mat of hair and blood, I knew her head had been crushed. My fear would not allow me to accept the obvious as my maternal instincts began to take charge of this hopeless situation.

"Wilbur, let's go to the hospital. Black Margaret, you take care of the kids. Pa, you get in touch with John Billy and have him meet us at Roper," I ordered them as I rushed around to the cab of the truck with Barbara in my arms. Wilbur helped me in and ordered Flash to the bed with the undelivered blocks of ice.

For a moment, everything was queerly quiet except for the gasping whimpers of Sarah. The silence was broken by the partly muffled engine of the Puckett ice truck. My screams, at least in my own mind, were able to drown out the reminding horrors of the truck's noise. Barbara's movement interrupted my crazed detachment as Wilbur double clutched the clutch-slipping transmission as he approached the graded incline of the Cooper River Bridge.

"She's alive, Wilbur. She's alive."

"No, ma'am. I think that is your new baby kicking," he said, trying to comfort me in some way.

It was the baby moving. So there I was, at the peak of the Cooper River Bridge, with one dead baby in my arms and another, only inches away, asking for life.

The people at Roper Hospital knew I was coming, but they didn't know I was bringing them one dead baby and one seeking delivery. There wasn't anything they could do for Barbara, but they sure had their hands full trying to take her away from me. I couldn't bear the thought of giving her up, even as my new baby was trying to come into this world, and he could no more wait than I could keep Barbara with me.

I kept pleading with the nurses to save my baby. They dishonestly vowed to do all they could to save her, but I wasn't talking about Barbara. I knew she was no longer with us.

They did save my new baby, but I don't remember a thing about it. I was at Roper for quite some time. However, they did permit me to attend the funeral. My recollection is spotty. My three aunts were there. They were in agreement with the sisters from the orphanage that Barbara's death was God's punishment for me marrying outside the Catholic Church. Sister Barbara was there. Since I had not seen her in years, I proudly offered that my Barbara was named in her honor.

Of course, John Billy's ma and pa, Iola, and Talmage made the drive from Tallapoosa. Paul came in from Pensacola, where he had been stationed after the war. It was the first time they had all been together in over ten years. Afterward, Iola decided to stay with us and help with the new baby, whom we had named Robert Talmadge after the doctor that delivered him and his uncle Talmage, but with a different spelling. A few years earlier, Iola had lost her own child in a similar accident when a drunken Deadeye Phagan allowed a load of pulpwood to fall on him.

After the funeral Mr. Bailey and Miss Sarah returned to Georgia, but Talmage and Paul stayed on for a while. They both felt that there was some unfinished business that needed tending.

What I learned about what happened after I returned to the hospital came from Sis, Iola, Black Margaret, and my pa. John Billy, Talmage and Paul never spoke a word of it. So what I have gathered is that

John Billy and his brothers got to drinking the day after the funeral. Sis heard Talmage tell John Billy and Paul, "We gotta get that black son of a bitch."

Of course, I knew that John Billy had quite the temper. I had witnessed it when he almost killed Deadeye Phagan for hitting Iola. I also knew that Talmage had not yet recovered from his war experience and was not yet stable. Paul, I think, was just following his brothers' lead. I just wish that I had been there to stop them.

John Billy found out that Flash was Black Margaret's cousin's boy. Black Margaret told me about them coming to see her. She told me, "Miss Mary, when Mr. John Billy and his brothers came to my house, they were all near blind drunk, and they all three had mean in their eyes. They asked me where that boy Flash was. I told Mr. John Billy that that boy was weak-minded and he did something only a weak-minded boy could have done. I told them it was a bad accident and God would see fit to punish that boy. They shouldn't go and do something that would get them in serious trouble. But they were paying me no never mind."

Black Margaret was right. They were not listening to her. John Billy found out where Flash lived. I think Mr. Puckett from the ice company told him. Anyway, they found him in Charleston and brought him back to the island.

Pa said that Talmage wanted to kill the boy with rocks, but John Billy wouldn't let him. Finally, Talmage told John Billy to leave the boy with him and Paul and they would take care of things. I don't think John Billy would have killed the boy, but Talmage would have viewed him as no more than Johnny's black puppy he had thrown off the porch.

I don't know if I will ever know what really happened. Black Margaret told me the boy disappeared from Charleston. He had relatives up in Philadelphia, she told me. The authorities did an effortless search of the back-water beaches but found neither hide nor hair of the young boy. They did find a body of a young colored man a day or two later at the bus yard where they kept the buses overnight. The young man's head had been crushed under the wheels of one of the city buses. The police told John Billy that they suspected him and his brothers, but with what he had just been through with the death of Barbara and the fact that his brothers had been in the war, it was understandable how something like this could happen to the colored boy. One policeman told John Billy, "The niggers are killing each other all the time. I guess one of them ran over this boy with a city bus."

On the island rumors were as plentiful as the sand bur stickers and just as annoying and often as painful. Months after Barbara's death, Black Margaret confessed that Flash, much bruised and battered, had indeed relocated to Philadelphia with his kin. However, with a sense of caution, the police did strongly suggest that Talmage and Paul go back to Georgia just in case someone wanted to create a stink.

Chapter 18

Murder on the Island

Talmage did return to Georgia. Paul was on leave from the navy and was due to return to Pensacola. He had met a south Alabama girl there and was going to propose to her when he returned.

After weeks of sedation and treatment at Roper Hospital, I was able to return home. Iola stayed on helping with the baby until I was able to get back to my full-time duties as mother to four young ones.

Meanwhile, John Billy had engaged a lawyer to seek liability compensation from Mr. Puckett's ice company. Mr. Puckett's insurance settled the suit for $25,000. On impulse, John Billy quit his job with the city bus company and purchased a service station on Highway 17 in Mount Pleasant, near Moultrie High School. As was his nature, he had no discussion with me about the purchase.

He just came home one day and told me, "We're moving to Mount Pleasant. I've purchased the filling station over by Moultrie High, and

I've found a house on Boundary Street. Once I get it painted, we will be moving there." I knew it was useless to protest.

However, something happened that made me realize that perhaps leaving the island was a good thing. There was a bad boding everywhere, and I wasn't sure I could take anymore of the ill curses being blown in from the Atlantic.

Angelina, Pa's alleged illegitimate child, started coming around more after Barbara's death. We saw her regularly over the years, but John Billy found her to be disquieting to say the least. I remember once she was over one June for a birthday party for Johnny. A sudden summer storm rolled up with thunder and lightning as the kids were playing in the yard. As we scurried the children inside, Angelina dallied in the rain, looking up at the squalling skies and seeming to find a kinship with the storm. I yelled at her to get in the house on the double-quick. She heeded my call, but ploddingly. As she reached the screen door, a bolt of lightning hit just as she gripped the metal handle. The mesh of the door lit up, and Angelina came off the porch hardwood about six inches. There were no tears. There was no sign of anguish. She said not a word but revealed something between a smile and a grimace.

"You keep an eye on that girl," John Billy told me. "I don't like her coming over here. She is downright spooky."

I agreed. There was something about Angelina—the way she appeared out of nowhere with her ever-present and annoying cold, black, no-teeth-showing grin. The barbaric way she toyed with her dog Will was off putting, as was her habit of showing up at mealtime but remaining mute throughout the meal.

I suppose I reached out to her out of charity. She was, after all, my supposed half sister. However, as much as I offered my heart to Angelina, she seemed to have no heart of her own to offer anyone. Gladys Snowden did her best to raise her, but she, too, noticed that Angelina was unlike other children. She called Gladys "Mother" and

Freddie Snowden "Father", as she had no clue that perhaps my pa and Annamarie Messina were possibly her real parents.

About the time Angelina had reached an early puberty, the Snowdens had taken in another child—their grandson from a daughter who was chasing a man, a soldier, from Natchez, Mississippi. He wanted nothing to do with the girl, and she wanted nothing to do with the child.

After the young boy arrived at the Snowdens', Angelina appeared regularly at our house. She appeared at breakfast. She appeared at lunch. She appeared at supper, but more often than not, John Billy made her go home. Gladys Snowden had a heart of gold and the compassion of Christ but was as poor as Job's turkey. An alms hunter's meal for a strange little girl was the least I could do for my destitute friend and neighbor who had taken in an outcast stray.

With John Billy's urging, I asked Gladys to keep Angelina at home at supper-time. I told her John Billy liked having the family together when he got home from work. Gladys agreed, but just as easily as the ghostly young girl could appear out of no-where to dine with us, she could also disappear from the not-so-watchful eyes of Gladys and Freddie Snowden.

One day, just before we moved to Mount Pleasant, Gladys came by asking if I had seen her grandson. I had not and told her so. She said that she had not seen him since just after breakfast. She and I walked to the back of our house to the back beach but saw no signs of the young boy.

Danny was a curly-haired, bright-eyed two-year-old. He loved Gladys, as she was a very doting grandmother. Gladys said she had last seen him before noon when he went out with Angelina to feed the rabbits.

Angelina told Gladys that Danny had gone back to the house after feeding their rabbits while she stayed outside to play with her dog, Will.

I suggested to Gladys that she put in a call to the police. The Charleston County Police sent out an officer who searched the backyard of the Snowdens'. Freddie was a junkman's hoarder. The Snowden yard was a shipload of rubbish. Rusted barrels, sheets of tin, unused boat scraps, and pipes and fittings from his plumbing were strewn across the yard. A sweat-free search turned up no sign of the boy.

After his search, the officer began to press Angelina about the boy's disappearance. She, while crying without tears, tendered a story of abduction and murder. She told the officer that a large bald man had entered the yard while they were feeding the rabbits. He had a nickel-plated pistol like you see in the movies. He offered her candy if she would go into the house to fetch a knife. When she returned, she claimed that he put Danny on the ground and stuffed his mouth with sweet potato vines to stifle his cries. After he cut Danny's throat from lobe to lobe, he stuffed him in a bucket that Freddie used to water his hogs and made her carry the bucket to the spot where he was hidden. She said that after he cut the boy's throat, he told her if she told anyone he would kill her and her family. She said she kept silent for fear that he would kill her ma and pa, meaning Gladys and Freddie.

The officer called for backup to help search for Danny and a detective to further question Angelina. In all, about seventy-five people turned out to search for Danny, but nighttime caught them and they had to return the following day.

The detective, at the suggestion of Gladys, called in one of Angelina's teachers to help with getting at the truth. Mrs. Howe, the teacher, said to Angelina, "I have always taught you to tell the truth. So tell me and this officer the truth about what happened to Danny."

Angelina changed her story. She said that she and the boy went out to feed the rabbits. She got a knife from the kitchen to cut sweet potato vines for the rabbits. On the way to the rabbit pen, Danny picked up a stick and hit her dog, Will. That made her angry, so when they got to the potato patch, she slit his throat, kissed him on the fore-head, stuffed him into the bucket, and dragged him over to some brush and covered him with tin "so the animals wouldn't worry him". She told the detective and Mrs. Howe that she loved Danny, but he had made her mad. She also admitted that she was jealous of him because Gladys and Freddie loved him more than they loved her.

By a judge's order, Angelina was committed to the state hospital in Columbia for observation. A grand jury would determine her fate afterward considering her sanity and if she should stand trial for murder. The doctors determined that she was sane but borderline mentally deficient. At last, and because of her age, she was placed in the girls' training school in Clinton.

The whole affair with Angelina spooked me. I was ready to leave Sullivan's Island. She had been in my home and played with my children. She could have just as easily slit the throat of Johnny, Joseph, or Sarah. Mount Pleasant felt like a new start.

Chapter 19

The Not-So-Pleasant Mount Pleasant

Changes were coming at me from all points on the compass—a new home, school changes for the kids. My pa had married Annamarie Messina, but was back home living with me within a month's time. He said he just couldn't live with Montella Zoccoletta another day. I'm not sure he had any gifts for the Italian tongue, but by his translation she was the "Nasty Bitch". I was not surprised at all when he returned. His old habits of living on someone else's dime could not escape him.

After Barbara's death, I witnessed a change in John Billy. He was always a beer drinker, but now he was tapping the harder stuff and drinking even more beer. His approach with the kids became over-bearingly strict. He would not allow them to sleep late on weekends. Spankings became more routine for the least of infractions.

One afternoon he came home from his new filling station, but I could tell his mind was still at the pumps, or on Goat Island, or maybe in Kalamazoo, Michigan. His posture confirmed a troubled spirit. Supper for me and him was joyless. Aside from the kids' usual rambunctiousness, not a word was spoken with any civility. A few hours after the meal, and as I was cleaning the table, I heard him ask Joseph and Johnny if they had seen his watch. He had purchased a watch with the funds won in our suit from the ice truck tragedy. They each denied playing with the watch, but he would not let it go.

"I set it on this table," he said to them, tapping at the table where he placed his loose change, car keys, and cigarettes when he came in from work each day. "Did y'all pick it up?"

"No, sir," they said in unison, but with a pang of fear in their voices.

"Don't lie to me. I put it right on the table. Did you take it outside when you went out to play after supper?" Before they could answer, he said, "Get back in that yard and find my watch."

The boys went to the yard. I could see that they were looking for the missing watch, scratching around in every crack and cranny in the sparsely grassed yard. Just as darkness settled in, he called them in to continue his interrogation. He asked them individually if they had taken the watch. Both boys again denied that they had. Tears began to well up in Joseph's eyes. John Billy saw that as an admission of guilt.

"What did you do with it?" he demanded.

"I don't remember," Joseph answered as he patted his pockets to see if the watch was there.

John Billy began to pull off his belt, giving Joseph time to think about where he had last had the watch. Joseph had no answer, and the strikes came. I walked over to the table to see if the watch had fallen to the floor. It had not, but when I opened the top drawer, there sat the watch, right where John Billy had placed it when he came home.

I picked up the watch and as I took Joseph by the hand, I said, "Here's your damn watch." As Joseph and I walked away I felt the strap of the belt strike me across my right shoulder.

"Don't you get smart with me."

Without hesitation I turned and said to him, "The Bible says to turn the other cheek when an enemy strikes you." I stuck out my face and said, "Why don't you hit me again? I've had nuns hit me harder than that."

He drew back but was intercepted by Johnny, who lit into him like a swarm of Carolina gnats. He pushed Johnny to the floor, picked up his cigarettes and lighter from the table and went off to the front porch, lighting a Camel as he closed the door.

I was to learn that apologies never came easy for John Billy Bailey. There was never an apology to me or the boys. The next morning he was off to the filling station, and at the end of the day, he came in as if nothing had happened.

Nothing more was ever said about the incident with the watch. There was a distance between us for sometime, but things gradually got better. The filling station wasn't thriving, but we were able to make ends meet. Meanwhile Pa was going down-hill. He developed a cough that was lingering.

To add to the bedlam of what was now our chaotic household, Sis had been living with us off and on as Morris Rape traipsed from one military assignment to another. It seemed he put in for every foreign post possible. When he was stateside, Sis would live with him at what ever post he was assigned. It might be Shaw Field in Sumter or Maxwell in Alabama or Robins in Georgia, but as soon as he could, he would put in for some foreign assignment. I think Sis was afraid of going overseas with him, and he doubtless didn't want her on board. They, by now, had two children of their own, conceived and birthed each time he came home from across the oceans. Morris, for now, was back in Japan, leaving Sis with two small children and an allotment check. John Billy was willing to take her in only because she was my sister and she was willing to share the allotment check for rent.

So here we were in Mount Pleasant—me, John Billy, and our four and a fifth on the way; Sis and her two; and my fading father. Yes, I was pregnant again with child number six, if you count Barbara. John Billy was working from the rise of the sun to the night's fall, or so I thought.

Sis began to pick up on rumors that Gabrielle De LaRue was spending much of her free time getting her fluids checked at John Billy's filling station. Gabrielle De LaRue was a clerk and jerk at the drugstore in Mount Pleasant where John Billy drew his daily blue plate special. She was a married woman with two of her own. Her husband was on the road most weeks selling life insurance policies throughout rural Carolina. The perfect storm could not be avoided, I suppose.

The suspicious tryst that began as a not-so-innocent flirtation soon led to a suspected full-bloomed betrayal. The unconfirmed deception lasted the length of my pregnancy. When Gabrielle became pregnant herself, the whispered rumors oscillated. Was it her husband's child? Was it John Billy's child? One charge was that the child belonged to the pharmacist.

It appeared that the rumor mill in Mount Pleasant was just as productive as it was on Sullivan's Island. I heard the rumors, but what was I supposed to do? Divorce was out of the question. John Billy would head back to Georgia, and I would be left with five children to raise on my own. My thoughts were of the orphanage and how I ended up there because my parents were not able to tend to my and Sis's needs when we were young. I didn't want that for my children. So I kept my mouth shut, and John Billy certainly wasn't talking. We had our child, Darlene, and Gabrielle had her baby, Jean Baptiste De LaRue.

In the early months of 1951, I began to notice that John Billy was getting a copious volume of letters from Tallapoosa, but by springtime the return address had changed to Villa Rica, Georgia. John Billy never shared the contents of the letters, even when I mentioned the change of the return address.

"Why are the letters from your ma and pa marked Villa Rica, Georgia, and not Tallapoosa?" I asked him.

"Oh, did I not tell you? They have moved to Villa Rica. Daddy was surveying some land and found this hundred-acre farm near Villa Rica. He got a good deal on the land, sold his farm in Tallapoosa to Viola and her husband, and moved to this new place. Talmage and his new wife are going to live with them and help run the farm."

"Talmage has a new wife?" I asked in total surprise.

"Oh yeah, I guess I didn't mention that either. Sorry, it must have slipped my mind," he said, but he quickly went back to the farm. "It sounds like a good piece of farmland. It has good soil and two open fields of bottomland. They plan on raising cotton and corn. Two mules and equipment came with the sale. It has a six-stall barn and a milk cow. There is electricity wired to the house, but the water is well water."

My heart plunged to my bowels. I kept an unbent face, not ushering in any inkling that I knew what was in the works. I knew then was not the time to discuss it, and most likely, there would never be a time to discuss it for John Billy. The move to Georgia was in the brew.

That summer Johnny and Joseph picked up a paper route with the News and Courier. Each day they rode the streets of Mount Pleasant, slinging papers at homes and businesses. John Billy took the better part of their earnings, since, by his estimation, it was due him for finding the job in the first place, and it was in his car that they delivered when he drove on rainy days.

My older three were looking forward to the transition from their island school to their new school in Mount Pleasant. We lived only a few hundred yards from Moultrie High School. The boys were especially looking forward to when they could one day sport uniforms for the Generals. When they played backyard football, they argued constantly about who would take on the role of Forest Calvert, the local high school star.

On the island the older two boys had lived the island life. They searched for pirates' gold. They championed bicycle marathons. They explored the abandoned bunkers from World War II with no more than a matchbook for light to guide them. Their fantasies had them ferreting along the coastline for German subs, fighting and capturing the Seminole chief, Osceola, and protecting the Charleston Harbor from either the British or the Yankees. Life for them was a romp, an idyllic existence.

Mount Pleasant, on the other hand, offered adventures of a different sort. Our home on Boundary Street abutted the colored section of the town. Our house was the last white folks' house before the colored neighborhood. In the segregated world of post-World War II Charleston, the white and colored boys got along famously. My boys introduced the colored boys to their beach game of what they called "half rubber." All that was needed was a rubber ball, which they cut in half, and a broomstick. They could make that ball sail and spin and dive just like Dizzy Dean. On a Sunday afternoon, all the neighbors, both white and colored, would gather to watch the kids play half rubber.

The other sport of passion for the boys was boxing. Without adult supervision, the backyard bantamweights would outline a ring with the half rubber broomstick, select a referee, lace up the much-too-heavy and worn gloves, and pair themselves by weight class. No matter his size, each pint-sized pugilist emulated the great heavy-weights of the time. The colored boys' chosen-one was Joe Louis and the white boys echoed Jack Dempsey. My two boys were well schooled in the sport of boxing. John Billy and his brothers, Talmage and Paul, when they were with us, felt the need to teach the boys to box. I must admit that I fancied the sport as well. Listening to the fights on the radio with my pa and John Billy gave me an appreciation for the sport.

My boys were not bad. In fact, Joseph was quite scrappy, but he had a tendency to cry easily. He would quite often beat his opponent but would come home with a mixture of blood and tears trickling down his nose and chin.

Joseph could hold his own against any of the colored boys, especially those close to his size, but there was one bullyboy who was older and bigger than all the others. He would only box the small boys and always beat them, but he always had an excuse when it came to fighting anyone near his size. There was not one of the neighborhood boys, colored or white, who was actually Red Ellers's size. He was a head taller than most of the others and had them by a fat twenty-five pounds. Joseph was the only small kid who would willingly don the gloves against Red Ellers, but the result was always the same—Joseph coming home crying to me that Red Ellers beat him up.

"Why do you fight him, then?" I would ask.

"Because I was afraid if I didn't fight him, he would beat me up."

After several tear-and-blood-stained bouts, I got fed up with Joseph coming home to me crying that Red Ellers had beaten him up.

"Don't come in here crying anymore. I am sick and tired of it. If you can't handle it, then just stay home," I scolded him. But then I added, after some thought, "You get back out there right this minute and give Red Ellers some of his own medicine, and don't come back here until you do."

More tears came, but Joseph went back out to face Red Ellers. Johnny later related this story to me.

Through his tears Joseph told Red Ellers, "My mama says that I have to whip you or I can't come back home."

Red laughed one of those exaggerated laughs of uncertainty. "What?" he asked.

"You heard me. I gotta give you a shellacking," Joseph said matter-of-factly.

"OK, crybaby. Let's put on the gloves, and I'll send you back to your mama blubbering like a whale."

"No gloves. We are going bare knuckle," Joseph said as he crouched down doing his best to parrot Willie Pep.

Johnny gave me the blow-by-blow description. Red Ellers charged, but was met with a volley to his fat belly. Red stepped away, already breathing heavily. Joseph stepped right, bobbing and weaving. Red followed, but Joseph sprang left and landed a cross on Red's ear. When Red reached for his stinging ear with his right hand, Joseph countered with a direct shot to Red's fat nose. Red grabbed his nose as the blood spewed between his fingers. Before Joseph could land his—in Johnny's words—"cooty grass," Red was on his knees. "I'm gonna tell my mama on you," he said to Joseph.

"Go ahead. I don't care. Bring her out here, and I'll whip her fat ass too," Joseph screamed at Red.

Johnny, beaming with pride for his little brother, ushered him home and told me what had happened. Joseph, meanwhile, was filling his smile with tears of triumph.

Joseph became a neighborhood legend. Respect came from both colored and white. He was the little boy who slew the Red Dragon. In fact, that became his moniker—Sir Jody, the Little Red Dragon Slayer. He wore it proudly, and we all began to use Jody as a testament to his bravery.

It was only a matter of time before the inevitable. Two eventualities triggered our fate. For one, Pa died. His lungs and kidneys failed him that fall. He had sent Johnny to Willie's Platter to pick up what he called his essentials. Willie's Platter was a sandwich-and-food store in the colored neighborhood where one could purchase incidentals. Neither food nor sandwiches were the incidentals that my pa found essential. Willie's Platter did a profitable business, after Prohibition ended, in the spirits business. Willie and his wife, Erlene, were horse traders who had extended the privilege of shopping at their establishment to my pa for a paint job he had done years earlier. Once my pa was unable to shop for himself, Johnny became his runner. On the day that Pa died, he had sent Johnny to Willie's Platter for some smokes and brew. When Johnny returned, he found Pa passed out on the floor of his bedroom.

My pa battled hostiles all his life. Some of his enemies were real, but many were not. His inflated aggressiveness was meant to compensate for his personal and perceived inferiority. He was most distrustful of those he saw as haughty, and for him most of Charleston was haughty. His polio leg was his rationale for viewing others as being condescending toward him. The chip on his shoulder was the size of one of his paint cans, yet it was the contents of those cans that brought him some bearing of relevancy. He was a master with the paintbrush. He was a perfectionist with his preparation, and his trim work was classic. He had the unique ability to paint a wall with horizontal ribbons that rivaled the most formal papered walls in Charleston. When mixing paint, he was in his element. He was an acrobat on the ladder in spite of his wasted legs. Charleston's gentility sought him out. He could have made a decent living with his craft had it not been for the Depression and his passion for the bottle. I knew I would miss him with feelings of bitterness and devotion. I also knew that his passing would bring about changes for which I was not ready.

The other fate changer for me and my family was the steady whispers from the Mount Pleasant townies about John Billy's affair with Gabrielle de LaRue. Her child, now two years old, was rumored to be the spitting image of John Billy. I don't know if that is true or not, but the rumors stung me and shamed John Billy. The not-so-unanticipated news finally came.

"I sold the filling station. I can't do much more than rotate tires, change oil, and gas up cars, and it is too difficult to keep a good mechanic around. A five-cents-an hour offer from somewhere else and they are gone. We are losing money. I can go back to driving the bus, if necessary," John Billy said, feeling me out on the idea of driving the bus again.

I knew that driving the bus was not his intent. Then it came.

"Daddy has offered the farm in Villa Rica. He is moving Talmage and his wife to the tenant house up the road. He and Mama have found a place between Villa Rica and Temple. Daddy said since we have three boys, we could best run the farm, and Talmage will be there to help. Daddy is gonna help with the first year's purchase of seed. He has a hog we can kill this winter and share the meat with him and Talmage. And there's the milk cow and the two mules," he reasoned, more to himself than to me.

"I thought you hated farming with your pa. Y'all can't get along. My boys don't know the first thing about plowing behind a mule, and I don't know the first thing about hog killing, and milking a cow, or anything else to do with farm work. The kids have school here and new friends. I'll get a job if need be," I rattled on with my own reasoning.

I knew the decision had already been made, and John Billy confirmed it when he said, "We are moving this weekend. I've asked Ted Simmons to drive his truck to move our larger things. Talmage and I will come back with Ted and get the rest of our stuff," he said, laying out his plans.

"But what about the kids? They have school," I protested.

"Well, we ain't gonna leave them here," he said sarcastically. "They have schools in Georgia," he added, with even more mocking.

I went into Pa's old room and cried. Then I began to pack. I told the kids about the move, then I cried some more. Aside from our honeymoon trip to Tallapoosa, I had never been out of Charleston County. Now I was making a permanent move to some godforsaken misery of a sharecropping backwoods town that didn't even have an American name.

Mary Margaret Knight (on right) and twin Bubba Knight.

Queen Street Catholic Orphanage

Delia Anthony LaVelle
1/23/1880-5/22/1944

Mary Margaret's mother - Delia LaVelle Knight.

Jakey Knight

Nora (Sis) and Mary Margaret

Mary Margaret (teen years)

John Billy and Mary Margaret with first born, Johnny.

Barbara (killed by an Ice delivery truck - January 1947.

John Billy's service station (purchased from Wrongful
Death settlement)

John Billy working WPA job during WWII.

Joseph, Johnny, Barbara, Sarah and Cousin Ellen playing on the Back Beach on Sullivan Island.

Life on Sullivan Island, circa 1942.

One of 3 litters of puppies.

Charley horse and the three amigos

Villa Rica farm (12 years after Mary Margaret's family
moved into town.

Mary Margaret and John Billy (approx. 1953)

Church Time: Back Row-Sarah, Jody, Mary Margaret, Johnny
Front Row-Robert, Darlene

John Billy, Mary Margaret & Sis (Nora's son Paul)

Miss Sarah and Mary Margaret on a rest stop headed to
"See Rock City"

John Billy's father, Isaac Walton Bailey

VILLA RICA, GEORGIA 1952-1959

Chapter 20

I'm No Farmer's Daughter

The drive from Charleston to Georgia was not as full of hope and promise for the future as my first venture into Georgia. There was an unknown that first visit. Then the novelty of the unfamiliar was unraveled for me by John Billy, leaving me unkindly primed for life in Tallapoosa. However, this Georgia journey was to be permanent. There was no fleeing back to Carolina. There would be no island citadel of inviting comfort.

John Billy spoke very little on the drive other than to thunder at the kids when they distracted him from his uncertainty. He knew he could farm, but his musing was, "Can I make a living from the unseen neck of Georgia woods?" He would never admit that he had reservations, but his face told no lies.

The convoy of our 1947 Ford and Ted Simmons's 1950 Ford pickup truck arrived in a pouring rain. The pitchy clouds hung overhead as a harbinger of impending gloom. Ted's pickup was saddled with a Joad-family load of bedding and furnishings. Our sedan was fraught with kids, so there was little room for anything of measure. The Ford's trunk held the closet's clothes and dressers' contents minus the dressers. The floorboards, both back and front, accommodated the incidentals from the kitchen and bathroom.

Just as Ted and John Billy began unloading Ted's truck, the rains ceased and the clouds broke. The peeking sun boosted our spirits, yet it created a misty overhang that seemed to corral the foul stink coming from the barn. This was not a Charleston stink of brine waters and fish hauls but a foulness of mule dung, hogwash, and chicken manure.

Our mattresses had been blanketed with military canvas ,which left them musty but not wet. This only added to the foulness of the countri-fied air. The sun would dry them before nightfall. The older boys, with Robert trekking behind, headed to the barn to explore. John Billy put an immediate halt to that sally.

"You boys get back here and help us unload," he insisted. They and I were assigned the sedan to unload while Ted and John Billy managed the heavier pieces.

Betwixt and between unloading clothes and kitchen implements and all the while keeping the kids from provoking John Billy, I scoured my new neck of the woods, trying to uncover the various sources of stink. I had no luck. The gamut of stench melded into one disgusting bouquet of rotten putridness. The manure from the barn, the swine swill from the porker's pen, the chicken litter everywhere, and the human excre-ment from the privy all blended into one mass of pungent permeation.

I suppose Charleston has its own aroma. Fish odor to the novice can be off setting. Brackish water is no more pleasant than mule manure. Pulpwood and paper mills can rival the best of any Georgia two-seater. But those were my smells. Those were the smells I grew up with. Those were the smells of Charleston.

Nightfall came as quickly as exhaustion for the kids. My and John Billy's bed was pieced together, but Ted and the kids bedded down on floor pallets. We had peanut butter and jelly sandwiches for supper before the kids and Ted retired to their pallets.

The next morning John Billy, Ted, and Talmage headed back to Charleston to retrieve the remainder of our belongings, or whatever he could fit into our Ford. No sooner had they left than I was visited by Talmage's new bride, Jerry. Jerry, of course, was the short account for Geraldine. She had wiry red hair and a body to match. Jerry, I discovered immediately, had three discriminating traits. She could talk the ears off a mule. She smoked like a Carolina paper mill, and she was not short on judgments.

Between deep draws from her Lucky Strike, she began to tell me about our new farm.

"Mary Margaret, you know that Talmage and I lived here before y'all came down from Charleston," she said.

"I know," I replied. "Thank you so much for moving to the smaller house. I don't think we could have fit my brood in there."

"Child, you got a lot to learn. We didn't move out. We were forced out. Old Man Bailey told us to get out to make room for you and John Billy. Talmage protested, but for what? Once Mr. Bailey makes up his mind, there ain't no argument," she stated matter-of-factly.

I could see the resentment in her eyes and hear the hurt in her voice.

"I am so sorry. I didn't know. John Billy didn't say anything about that," I apologized.

"Of course he didn't say anything to you. He's a Bailey. I know you didn't know. What I've learned about the Bailey men is that they are right closemouthed when it comes to sharing with their womenfolk. Mr. Bailey may be the most tight-lipped of them all. I suppose John Billy is just like that. Talmage is, but I don't cotton to that from a man," she said, and then followed that with, "Hey, have you found the facilities yet?"

"No, and I gotta go real bad," I replied. without commenting on the passionless personalities of the Bailey men.

"Follow me, then," she said.

The privy was about thirty yards back of the house, just past an old black walnut tree that had scatterings of ripened nuts at its foot. The outhouse was nestled behind a stand of bamboo canes that seemed to be growing at will.

"You will enjoy the walnuts, but it is hard as hell to get at the meat. These canes are just a nuisance, not good for anything but making fishing poles and hiding the out-house," she shared, trying to help me with the subtleties of becoming a farmer's wife. "Well, come on in. You have a two-seater," she added.

"The only thing you have to worry about is the wasps in the summer and the snakes," she said as she handed me a page from a mail-order catalog.

I looked at her puzzled-like.

"Toilet paper, my dear," she said, while at the same time pointing to a trough of corn cobs. "Back up. You ever heard the term 'rougher than a cob'?"

"Oh my word. Doesn't that smart?" I asked.

"You'll get used to it. Beats your fingers. C'mon, let me introduce you to your farm critters," she said as she pulled up her undies.

Walking past the bamboo canes, we took a left and were soon met with the foul oder of the hog pen.

"This is Sow Sow. Come winter we will be having a hog killing," Jerry said, as she scratched Sow Sow behind the ears. "Feed her all your table scraps. She will eat most anything, though."

As we moved on toward the barn, we found ourselves surrounded by chickens. They were milling about, blind to our presence except for a large red rooster.

"That rooster is getting mean. He's flogged me a couple of times," Jerry said while showing me her shins. "I've about had enough of him. I'm gonna let him partner with some dumplings soon enough. Some people don't like eating roosters, but if you get them young enough, they are not so tough. They taste just like chicken," she laughed.

I moved to her left, allowing Jerry to contend with the rooster should he decide to attack.

"They are just like any animal," she said. "They are territorial, and they will protect their girls. We keep them around to ward off dogs or foxes or coyotes.

"They will even kill a snake if they find one around the henhouse. We also have to keep them to fertilize the eggs, but if you just want breakfast and baking eggs, you don't need that old boy. Don't show any fear, and he will probably leave you alone. You'll have to go out to the hen-house each day to collect the eggs. Once he gets used to you doing that, he will leave you alone. If you try to hit or kick him, he'll see that as a challenge to his manhood and come fighting back. Like I said, this one needs to be on the supper table. John Billy can find you another one that's not so ornery. Oh, yeah, and you'll have to feed them. I feed them twice a day. The scratch is good for better eggs, but they spend the day roaming around eating worms and grubs. Keep an eye out for rats. They will come and eat the grains in the scratch. That will be a good job for the boys—rat killers."

As I was soaking up all Jerry's farm wisdom, we moved on to the barn.

"How do you know so much about running a farm?" I asked Jerry.

"Shoot, girl, I was brought up on a farm. I had three brothers, and I could out-work everyone. I was the best, and they had to learn from me."

The barn, to my amazement, was still erect but had a slight lean to the left. I could not gauge how on earth this gray clapboard building was not in shambles. There was a wagon-sized opening at each end with stalls on either side. There was a second floor that had to be accessed by a makeshift ladder that was nailed to the wall. On closer inspection than the evening before, I found the smell was not much better than that of the pig pen we had visited and, both made my nose run.

"That's Jane and Red," Jerry said, pointing out the two mules stalled and eating some concoction of grain.

"They do all the real work around here. Jane is the sweetest mule you will ever find. She does her job with no complaints. Whatever you want her to do, she will do it. Red, on the other hand, is the meanest SOB in Douglas County. He is muleheaded, stubborn, and hell-bent on making everyone's life miserable. They are kinda like you and John Billy," she said, breaking out into a howl of laughter.

I smiled, knowing that she was right about that.

She continued on, "The boys may not be able to handle Red at first. She will try to bite and kick them, but once she is harnessed with the plow, she will do her work. When she comes in after plowing all day, she will bite and kick again as the collar and harness are removed. It is the darnedest sight you ever saw. Talmage could control her. John Billy will be able to and maybe your oldest once he gets the hang of it."

Jerry and I stood in the side yard and surveyed my new homeplace. She then gave me the overall picture.

"You got about a hundred acres here. Straight back of the barn is the largest section. It goes back to a good-sized creek with a swimming hole the kids will love. We call it Slick Rock Creek. It has a sliding rock waterfall that's a lot of fun. Me and Talmage have gone skinny-dipping there. The falls are so slick they don't even skin up my butt. That's good bottom land. Over to the right is the Weller farm. They have a boy about the age of yourn, but they don't do much with their land. They are getting on in age, and the boy is lazy. Across the road from the front of the house are a few acres that would be good for peanuts, or watermelons or sweet potatoes. Across that other road there is where our house is, if you want to call it a house. There is some good bottomland there as well and a good stand of trees that John Billy might be able to sell to the pulpwooders if he's a mind to and the old man gives his permission. Talmage has a still down on the creek on our side of the road. Mr. Bailey came nosing around one day and found it. He asked me if I knew who had built it. I acted as shocked as he was and told him I had no idea. He called the revenuers, and they busted it up. Talmage had it running again in a few months. He just makes enough for us for medicinal purposes," she ended, with a slap on her knee and a roaring belly laugh.

By this time the kids were up and stirring. Jerry helped with breakfast and showed me the finer skills of using the woodstove. We had eggs and pancakes using the flour and syrup I had brought along from home and fresh eggs from the layers that Jerry had robbed before we came inside.

Jerry stayed awhile after breakfast, and we chatted. I should say she chatted. I listened, but she had so much advice to offer me. I could not bear to see her leave.

I invited her to spend the night. She could see that I was fearful of spending my first night in Georgia alone with the kids. She accepted with "Sure thing—let me go home and tidy up, and I will help you with supper when I get back."

Chapter 21

Hello, Swimming Hole; Goodbye, Atlantic Ocean

Jerry stayed over the following day while we waited for John Billy and Talmage to return from Charleston. She helped me scour the farmhouse. We washed baseboards, swept cobwebs from the kids rooms, mopped the house throughout, and polished what little furniture we had.

The guys drove in around three in the afternoon. John Billy's car was loaded but not packed.

"Where is Ma's etagere?" I asked as I nosed around in the Ford. "And her nightstand?

"We didn't have room. I had to sell the things that wouldn't fit. I gave the chest to Ted for helping us move," he said coolly.

Tears welled up in my eyes. Those pieces were all I had left that connected me to my ma, but John Billy didn't seem to care. They were just an inconvenience for him to cart back to Georgia.

John Billy," I heard Jerry say, "those particular belongings were important to Mary Margaret. They were her mother's, for Christ's sake."

John Billy snapped her a look that would croak a bull-frog. "Mind your own business."

"My business is what I make my business," Jerry responded, determined not to be bullied by anyone, much less one of the Bailey boys.

"Jerry, don't say anymore. What's done is done," Talmage advised but did not dare demand.

Jerry's face turned as red as her hair. She turned to me with an apologetic head-shake and scowl. Then she turned to Talmage.

"Talmage, let's go," she insisted.

"I'll be right up. I'm gonna help John Billy unload," Talmage said with some misgivings.

"Suit yourself," Jerry replied as she stomped off across the yard.

The following day John Billy had the boys up at daybreak. He took them out to the barn to demonstrate the fine art of cow milking. Then he had them gather kindling for the woodstove so I could fry up some eggs. For the first week, the routine was the same—milk the cow, gather wood, draw water from the well, and then spend the remainder of the day clearing off the property surrounding the house. It was obvious that Talmage had not spent much time tidying up the place. Johnny and Jody were each given a sling blade, while John Billy manned a scythe to manage the denser vegetation. There were all manner of wild plants, some of which I knew from our gardens back in Charleston. There were others that seemed particular to the Georgia red clay. There were thistles, plantains and chickweed. Stands of briars were everywhere. Rabbit tobacco, wild onions, wild carrots, and scarlet sumac were also scattered about. Brown sedge was everywhere. The boys were swamped by the salad of wild vegetation. The clippings were piled up to dry out along with any other bits of rubble, limbs, and trash that were laying about. Once they dried out they would be burned.

My three school-aged kids were allowed a week off before they would be registered in the Villa Rica schools. John Billy presented the interruption as a reward for their cooperation while we made the move from Charleston, but it was more that he wanted them on the farm to help with all the work that needed to be done.

The years spent on the farm were a medley of adventures and escapades. The hard times were a test of my patience, my strength, and ultimately my faith. The good times were charged with memories forged for a lifetime. The memories, both spotless and spotted, were souvenirs of our years on the farm.

Sundays were a day of rest except for the essential assignments that come with farmstead living. The cow had to be milked, and the mules and chickens fed. Water had to be drawn for bathing and cooking. None of that ever stopped. On our first Sunday on the farm, John Billy wanted to take the family on a walking tour of the place. Talmage had given him a general layout, but John Billy wanted to have some personal assessment so he could design his master plan for spring planting.

All the kids wanted to see the slick rock on the creek that Jerry had told them about. Since it was just beyond the south bottoms, we made for there first. It was not an easy trek to the creek. We passed through the shot-gun of the barn and across the red clay and mostly grassless pasture. At the far end of the pasture was a stubble of scrub pines trying to compete with dwarfish hardwoods. A small creek bed ran amongst the struggling trees, but there was little flow to this creek. Mostly it was just a soggy bog that required gingerly steps to avoid the mire and muck.

Beyond the struggling streamlet and the copse of unsuccessful trees was a wild plum orchard. The plums were just past the ripening stage, and most were on the ground, spotted brown and with worms.

However, I could tell that come next season we could make use of them if I could get Jerry to teach me to make plum jelly.

Coming out of the plum orchard, we began to hear the roar of the falls, and we could smell the distinct pungency of the earthy dankness. The smell was not totally unlike the smell of the tidal flats at low tide, but less briny. The falls were surprisingly long and emptied into a pool hole as large as some of the beach tide pools on Sullivan's Island.

John Billy asked the boys, "Do y'all want to take a swim?".

Johnny said, "We don't have our suits"

"Don't need them here. Just skin down and jump right in."

I made the girls turn their backs while the boys disrobed, and we moved to a shallow puddle with our backs to the boys as they frolicked in the swimming hole. The pool seemed to be about four feet deep at the bottom of the falls. Johnny and Jody both climbed the slope to the top of the graded falls. It was at least a thirty-foot pitch from top of the falls to the chin-deep hole. After a splash around, the boys headed back to the top. As Jody climbed from the pool to mount the rocks to begin his ascension on all fours back to the top, I heard Johnny say, "What are those black things on your legs? Hey, they are on your back too."

"Leeches!" I screamed and immediately jumped into the pool, yanked Joseph off the rocks and started slapping at the suckers that I knew were sucking the lifeblood from his body. John Billy was on the bank paralyzed in laughter.

Recovering, he said, "They won't hurt you as long as you don't leave them on too long. Just pull them off. Now we know where to come for fish bait. They're great for crappie and catfish. Besides, they will go away once you start using the rock slide more often."

Johnny began to pull his off and toss them on the bank toward his sisters. I swatted him on the bottom, but the water broke my swat. Meanwhile, Jody, crying and laughing at the same time, was cautiously scraping off his leeches with a stick.

No sooner had we become leech-free than we heard Sarah scream-ing and pointing. John Billy seemed a little more concerned than he had been with the leeches. He bounded off the bank to see that Sarah was pointing at a cottonmouth that was sunning itself on a nearby slab of rock. He picked up a dead limb and proceeded to pound the rock, the tree limb, and the snake into a state of annihilation. Sarah was fro-zen, but Darlene and Robert both fell into the pool in their scramble to get away from the snake kerfuffle and to get to me. Johnny grabbed Darlene by her hair and pulled her to safety. I pulled Robert up from under the now-disturbed water and dragged him to the sandy flat.

All had to applaud the killing of the snake, but I was eager to vacate the perilous woods. Our excursion to explore our farmland ended with six soaked souls and one dry chuckler.

Returning to the house, I filled the galvanized wash-tub with well water for Darlene to bathe. Sarah did a wash-cloth bath since she was the only child not to plunge into the waters of Slick Rock Creek. John Billy took the three boys to inspect the bottomland south of the house.

Johnny and Jody returned about an hour later. They were both shouting and in somewhat of a panic.

I stuck my head out the door and asked, "What are you two raising such a ruckus about?"

"Mama, Robert fell in the well. He was trying to get a dipper of water and just fell in," Jody screamed.

My heart sank. I couldn't bear losing another child. I couldn't go on. I wouldn't go on. I ran toward the well.

"Where is your daddy?" I screamed at Johnny.

"He's in the outhouse," he replied.

"Hurry! Hurry! Go get him. Now!"

Johnny and Jody started laughing, and I saw Robert coming out of the barn with a sheepish look on his face. He didn't know whether to laugh with his brothers or cry with me. I immediately went to the burn pile and got the biggest hickory I could find. I tore into Johnny, and when I tired, I lit into Jody. With each lick I gave them, I bawled, "Don't you ever do that again."

John Billy came from the outhouse, hitching up his pants, to see what the clatter was about.

"These boys told me that Robert had fallen into the well," I said breathlessly.

"We're sorry," they said in one voice. "We were just joking."

John Billy took the hickory from me and began to whale on the boys some more. I picked up a crying Robert and reeled my way to the house. I fell onto the porch, too exhausted to move any further. Seeing me, John Billy stopped switching Johnny and Jody. He came to my side and helped me to our bed.

I knew the boys were just funning, but the death of Barbara was just too fresh in my memory. Losing a second child would have crushed me. The mere thought reminded me of how fragile life could be and that this place in Georgia was rife with perils from which I had to protect my children.

Chapter 22

Hog-Killing Time in Georgia

During our honeymoon time at Mr. Bailey and Miss Sarah's home in Tallapoosa, I didn't digest how profoundly regimented life on a farm could be—from the feeding of the chickens to the milking of the cow to the time for meals, there was no variation. Those tasks had to be taken care of before all else. The two older boys were adapting without much fuss to their chore list. There was the occasional kicked-over bucket of milk, mostly on Jody's part because he had not learned yet that he had to dominate the cow. His timidity and lack of command allowed the cow a sense of control.

Sundays, however, tendered liberties that were not a part of the monotony of farm life. More often than not, we took a visit across town to Mr. Bailey and Miss Sarah's, but after a while the visits became another part of the ritual. The one positive for me was that I did not have to prepare Sunday's dinner.

The Baileys' new home was an old farm place that was no longer operational. The barn remained empty, and the pastureland was
overgrown. Mr. Bailey was by now too old to farm, which was why
he conscripted John Billy to do his service on our farm. Mr. Bailey's
new place had been a milk farm in its heyday, but that was years prior.
Adjacent to the main house were two milk houses which Mr. Bailey
converted to rentals. In fact, he rented one of the houses to John Billy's
sister, Iola. The houses were no more than glorified barns with a woodstove. Iola did her best to dress up the place with curtains, but it was
like putting earbobs and a bonnet on the pig we were going to slaughter
soon. Iola divided her one-room milk house using the drain trough that
ran down the middle of her floor—living room on one side and bedroom on the other, and of course the kitchen was the woodstove.

The main house was infested, as was the house in Tallapoosa, on its
back side with honeybees. The lath and plaster were ideal for housing
bees. I imagine that the walls were dripping in honey. Miss Sarah was
forever finding deceased bees through-out her house. The upper level
of the house, which no one used, was a memorial to the fallen bee. Miss
Sarah took me up there once to show me the house. I couldn't step two
feet without crunching a rigor-mortified drone or worker.

Like many of the columned two-storied homes of an earlier time,
the house had an entrance divided by a wide flight of stairs that led
to bedrooms upstairs. On the main floor there was a bedroom or
parlor on the right, but for Miss Sarah it was just empty space. They
lived solely on the left side of the house. The door on the left from the
stair entranceway led to a living room that was oppressively hot. This
room was the only heated room in the house, unless one counted the
woodstove in the kitchen—and it was heated by an upright gas heater
inserted into the firebox of the old fireplace.

The living room fed into a smaller yet longish sleeping room that
separated the living room from the kitchen. There was a bed on either

side of the protracted sleeping quarters making it impossible to use for anything but sleeping.

Compared to the other two rooms, the kitchen was expansive. There was a cabinet for everything—dishes, utensils, pots and pans. There were bins for flour, sugar, potatoes, and onions and a sizable spice rack filled with more seasonings than a colonial Carolina spice ship. Miss Sarah had an ample-sized flour table with drawers and foldable wings. Her kitchen was a baker's envy. It was from Miss Sarah that I learned to make biscuits and spice cookies.

Off from the kitchen was an alcove that served as the dining room. There was ample room for even our large family to comfortably sit for a Sunday dinner. Exiting from the kitchen was a small mudroom that led to the rear entrance and to the breeding grounds of the honeybees.

I asked Miss Sarah once if the honeybees bothered her.

"Naw," she said. "Unless they handpick me as a bed mate."

It was these Sunday jaunts to my in-laws' that led to our attending church in Villa Rica. The Pleasant Grove Baptist Church was only a short ride from the Baileys' place. John Billy felt that since our kids were of an age at which they might reap the benefits of an organized religion, we might as well stop off at the Pleasant Grove Baptist Church before our Sunday repast at the Baileys'. John Billy never bothered with asking me if I wanted the kids raised Baptist or Catholic, not that it mattered, since there wasn't a Roman Catholic church within miles of Villa Rica, Georgia.

I preferred the Catholic option because that was what I knew. That was how I was raised. The kids did attend Stella Maris Catholic Church on Sullivan's Island on special occasions like Christmas, Palm Sunday, and Easter or whenever they had special programs for kids. Even John Billy would attend on Christmas and Easter, but he wasn't moved toward religion when we were in Charleston. I think being near his ma and pa and having five kids pressured him a bit to seek religion—that, and his past dalliances in Mount Pleasant after Barbara died may have led him to seek redemption. There is nothing like drinking, smoking, and fathering bastard children to make one seek atonement.

The Pleasant Grove Baptist Church was our best choice. Mr. Bailey's Hard-Shell Baptists seemed a bit too primitive for my liking. I did attend a church's revival nearer to our farm at the behest of a neighbor. John Billy called the attendees Holy Rollers and laughed when I told him I was going.

It was one of the tent revivals that evidently were popular in this part of Georgia. The tent was set up in my neighbor's pasture. When I arrived, I was greeted by thunderous singing and a lady handing out fans, each attached to what appeared to be a large Popsicle stick and a picture of Jesus that looked like Sterling Hayden with a hank of hair flowing to his shoulders.

The sermon was about the Tribulation. The preacher saw the war and the bomb of fire and the hardships in Europe and Japan and the worldwide famine as signs that the end was near. He preached and gyrated and sang. His every sentence concluded with an emphatic "ah". Sweat poured from his brow. People were running up and down the sawdust-covered aisles shouting with grunts, tics, and rolling tongues. Some were even prostrate in the sawdust, twitching like one of the hens John Billy had decapitated for a meal. I expected Jesus to lift a tent flap at any moment and gather us all for the homecoming.

I was exhausted at the sermon's end. My friend asked, "Did you feel it?"

I was honest with her: "Yes, I felt something."

What I felt was uncomfortable. I couldn't wait for my exodus from this canopied sideshow, but the preacher man was not finished. Next came the healing. People of all ages and sizes limped and dragged themselves to the front. Some were led by family and some were pulled. The preacher placed his hand on the impaired people one by one, beseeched Jesus to heal them, and then palm-punched them into the waiting arms of some Gabby Hartnett wannabe. Most shouted, arms flailing, limps and lumps apparently gone.

The service ended with a prayer that lasted about as long as the healing service. The preacher doomed us all to an eternal inferno, to perdition, and then asked if anyone wanted to join him in being safe and secure from all alarms. My neighbor nudged me to go forward, but I pretended to be in an invocation of my own and ignored her urging.

On the thankfully short ride home my sister—well, she called me her sister, but I didn't feel the kinship—asked if I wanted to return the next night.

"The preacher is going to explain the book of Revelations," she said excitedly.

"Thank you, but I think I've had enough revelations to last me awhile," I said to her as I escaped her car.

John Billy greeted me with, "Did you get to handle the cottonmouths?"

"No. They save that for the grand finale on Sunday," I said. "I am worn to a frazzle. I'm going to bed. Just ignore me if I scream in my sleep."

So for the time being, the Pleasant Grove Baptist Church was our refuge. It was conservative Southern Baptist with a preacher who didn't yell, and the most excitement came from the junior choir singing "Do Lord."

The autumns in Georgia, I found, fought a dogged battle to stave off Old Man Winter. During the armistice between the two, when it was nippy but not polar, it was hog- killing time, and it was just in time to provide a Thanksgiving ham. Hog-killing time, I discovered, was a festive family affair. Mr. Bailey and Miss Sarah came—he to supervise, she to work. Jerry and Talmage joined in, as both were aficionados of hog-killing. Iola, I found out, was as skilled with a knife and cleaver as

John Billy and Talmage. Johnny and Jody were there for the schooling and to do the legwork.

Sarah would help me and Miss Sarah with the details, and the two smaller kids were left to entertain themselves.

Before Talmage took the honor of actually killing the hog, there was prep work to be done. The men had already had a fire going under a large tub that Mr. Bailey had brought along. Johnny and Jody had drawn water from the well to fill the tub and were assigned the task of keeping the tub filled as it boiled away. Miss Sarah and I were busy sharpening the cutting tools—knives of various sizes and a butcher's hatchet.

We all gathered around the pen to watch Talmage do the actual killing. John Billy scratched the ears of the hog to get his attention. Talmage took aim between the hog's eyes. I must admit that I looked away before the shot was fired, but the echo of the rifle shot and the squealing of the hog were forever etched in my mind. I could not help but reflect on what Talmage must have endured and suffered while fighting the Japanese. I could only imagine that the soldiers' squalls as they were dying in battle were as dreadful as this dying pig's.

The hog was lifted by the men and my boys to a sled pulled by Jane and dragged to a makeshift hanging rack. Chains were attached to the hogs hind legs, and then he was lifted off the ground by a pulley. A large tub was placed under the hog, and then his Tweedledee and Tweedledum were cut off. John Billy cut the hog from his poop hole to his chinny chin chin. The hogs innards gushed into the tub with a gelatinous flop. The aroma was rank. I had helped Ma gut and clean her chickens before, but this stench could have gagged a maggot.

Then John Billy and Talmage hauled the gut bucket over to a table that was the work station for me, Jerry, and Miss Sarah.

Jerry began to separate the parts for keeping, which was just about everything in the blood bucket.

"I just love hog liver," she said as she tossed the liver aside. "Mary, we'll make chitlins from these," she said as she pulled out the ribbon of intestines "but we gotta clean them real good first. Don't want no poop germs."

Jerry was grabbing parts left and right. "You can make sweetbread from these, but most people don't like sweetbread from hogs. I'll feed these to my hounds," she said as she tossed the unidentifiable organs into a bucket she had brought along just for that purpose.

Jerry said to us all, "The Filipinos use the blood to thicken their sausage. Heck, some even make blood soup. Now the brains are good with scrambled eggs. We'll get the brains when we are finished with the body. Tongue, now I like cow's tongue, but I'm not much for a pig's tongue. Some people even eat the male's balls, but not so much from mature pigs. Now we will pickle the feet and snout."

Jerry didn't slow down once she got started. I think part of her tribute to the hog innards was to teach but a greater part was to entertain. Miss Sarah said little but shook her head and grinned as Jerry went on with her tutoring.

All the while Jerry was lamenting the ill fate of the hog's innards, the menfolk removed the head of the hog and shifted the hoist so that the hog could be scalded in the boiling water. Miss Sarah explained that the scalding made it easier to remove the hair by scraping. Since I had plucked chickens for my ma, I understood the need for the boiling water to loosen the hair. When I thought about it, the hog killing was pretty much the same as preparing a chicken but on a much larger scale.

Mr. Bailey directed John Billy and Talmage on the actual butchering of the hog. The meat was divided four ways, with me and John Billy getting the lion's share because we had seven mouths to feed. We had, or I should say Mr. Bailey had, a secondhand freezer he had purchased when he first moved to Villa Rica. The freezer was rickety, and the plug spit fire on occasion. We kept it on the back porch, what with it being a fire hazard and all.

Jerry and Iola were busy with the small intestines, boiling them for making chitlins. After the intestines were thoroughly cleaned, they were cut into smaller pieces. Miss Sarah had a cast-iron skillet going to fry up some crackling as a treat for the kids and the men.

The entire process was coming at me so fast I wasn't sure I grasped it all, particularly how to turn this raw meat into a meal. I was sure I could handle the bacon and ham, but when Miss Sarah and Iola and Jerry started talking about cracklin' cornbread, hog jowls, streak-o-lean, pickled feet, and making sausage, I was as out of place as a penguin on Thanksgiving. Miss Sarah and Iola offered to guide me through the complexities of hog cuisine if I would come to Miss Sarah's on the day after Thanksgiving.

John Billy agreed to keep the kids that Friday. He dropped me off at his parents' house with the understanding that Mr. Bailey would bring me home later that afternoon. I found that I was quite good at making cracklin' cornbread, but Miss Sarah had to remind me that real corn bread did not contain sugar. "Sugar is for cookies," she said.

The day was well spent. I picked up farmer cooking tips—the main one being that one should place fatback in most everything for the flavor. Miss Sarah and Iola promised that next harvest they would teach me to make muscadine and plum jelly and show me how to put up our vegetables when they came in during the summer.

On the ride home with Mr. Bailey, he asked how I was enjoying Georgia. I told him about the leeches and snake at the swimming hole. He assured me that the ticks and gnats in the summer were a much bigger nuisance than snakes and leeches.

He took me on a tour of Villa Rica, which was no more than a U-turn across the tracks. Villa Rica, he said, was a gold-mining town at one time, but when the gold mines panned out and the rails began to dominate transportation, the town moved from the gold mines to the rail tracks. Like most rail towns, it was divided by tracks. On one side of the tracks was the old town, the original settlement, and on the other was the newer part that grew as the town grew. He said that the man who started Coca-Cola, Asa Candler, was from Villa Rica. The south part of Villa Rica was a row of businesses and markets. Mr. Bailey took me by a newly built doctor's office and a very small hospital on the Carrollton Highway. It took us about ten minutes to tour the city. It was a far cry from Charleston.

Our place, Mr. Bailey's farm, was about three miles east of the downtown and south off Highway 78 a few more miles. When we turned off 78, the road was rutted and dirt. There was one store at the intersection near Highway 78 and then a spotting of farmhouses and shacks. Just past the store, I spotted a woman walking with a bag in her arms. I assumed she had been to the store. Just as we approached her, I realized it was Jerry.

"Mr. Bailey," I said. "Isn't that Jerry? We should pick her up."

He ignored me. I waved at her, assuming we would pull over to give her a lift. She waved back at me, I think also hoping that we would stop.

Mr. Bailey drove on. I knew he had heard me, and there was no way he could have missed Jerry's ginger hair.

When we got to our place, I asked him, "Mr. Bailey, why didn't you pick up Jerry?" I expected some indefensible excuse like "We didn't have room" or "I didn't see her."

He looked me in the eye and said, "I didn't want to." No more, no less, just "I didn't want to."

I sat on the steps and cried as he left, knowing that he would have to pass her again on his one-lane exit from our place. I waited for her.

"I'm so sorry. I told him it was you. He just wouldn't stop," I said to her through my tears.

"Not your fault," Jerry said with no sign of a tear. "He is a hard man. That will never change. Better get used to it."

Early that spring, just before planting time, Jerry and Talmage told me and John Billy that Talmage was reenlisting in the military. He was joining the air force, and they would be moving to Savannah, Georgia. John Billy was devastated. He was losing his right-hand man, and I was losing my only female companion, except for the Bible thumping lady up the way, and now the farm was falling into his lap completely. Within the week Jerry and Talmage were gone, and I had never felt more lonely in my life.

Chapter 23

Rat-Killing Time in Georgia

Even though we now had Talmage and Jerry's share of the hog we had killed and we had pullets we could count on, John Billy felt we needed to supplement our diet with gamier meats. He purchased—or horse traded, I should say—for each of the boys and himself a shotgun. He himself got a 12-gauge and the boys each got a 20-gauge. He also obtained a .22 rifle for killing the barn rats and squirrels. John Billy explained to me and the boys about the gauges on shotguns. I thought the higher the gauge, the more powerful the gun, but in fact, the opposite is the rule. He said the boys were safe with the 20-gauges and the kick back would not knock them down.

John Billy started collecting dogs to go along with the hunting weapons. He wanted the boys to train them, so he picked up both beagles and bird dogs and one redbone coon dog. It wasn't long before we were knee deep in puppies. At the upper-most count, we had twenty-one dogs after each female birthed a litter just weeks apart. The redbone killed two of the beagle puppies who tried to share his table scraps, so John Billy swapped him and several of the other puppies to a neighbor for a horse. He said he had to give twenty-five dollars to boot to get a fair trade on the horse. I didn't know what a "to boot" was, but he assured me that it was a good horse trade.

The horse trade was necessary, or so John Billy thought. The mule Jane was getting long in the teeth, so the plan was to make the horse a plow horse. The horse's name was Charley. Charley was the most gentle of animals in God's green pastures. The kids could ride him, walk behind him, and even walk under him. He enjoyed their company and the apples they fed him.

Come spring planting, John Billy determined that it was time to fashion Charley into a suitable replacement for the failing Jane. He had already harnessed both Jane and Red at various times that winter when he was moving heavy objects like stones to rebuild our front steps. Jane was easy to harness. Red, as Jerry had said, was difficult, but once she was hitched up, she was ready to work. To watch Red work was to watch a performance. The more demanding the work, the more she rose to the challenge. She was an artist. She anticipated the plowman's every need. Jane, on the other hand, was simply steady. No showman at all was she, but in her prime, we were told by Mr. Bailey, at the end of the day she was Red's equal.

Charley balked immediately when John Billy approached him with the plow collar, pulling away on the bitless rope bridle. John Billy gave an earnest yank, and Charley settled for a moment, but as soon as John Billy raised the collar, Charley bolted. The horse was having none of it. John Billy took the harness strap and began lashing at Charley. My boys moved back when they saw the anger erupting from their daddy. John Billy was flushed with a frenzied fury I had not seen.

"Johnny, come here. Hold this rein," he screamed at our oldest.

Johnny hesitated, but a swipe with the leather strap got him moving. As soon as Johnny grabbed the rein, Charley settled. John Billy approached our back porch and told me to throw him the broom. I didn't hesitate. He broke the broomstick in half and threw the bristled head back at me.

As he headed to the barn, passing Johnny and Charley, he said, "Don't let go of that horse."

Tears were welling up in Johnny's eyes, and Jody was in a full chorus of wails. I called Jody to the porch to ease his grief and to get him as far away from his daddy as possible. John Billy returned from the barn with a bullwhip made from barbed wire and the broken broom handle. He grabbed the rope from Johnny's hand and began to strike the horse, ripping him open with each lash. I suppose John Billy's aim was to horsewhip Charley into submission. With each strike Charley either reared, flailing his front hooves at John Billy, or kicked at him with his powerful hind legs. If the horse had made contact, John Billy would have died on the spot. Soon, Charley managed to liberate himself from John Billy's white-knuckled grip and sprinted out behind the out-house.

John Billy turned to a wooden and mortified Johnny. "Go get your horse," he said. He turned to Jody on the porch. "Help your brother, and quit crying, or I'll give you something to cry about."

The boys tracked after Charley. They found him eating grass some distance from the house. They let him pasture awhile to give their daddy time to settle. Charley followed the boys to the barn, where they stalled him.

As John Billy approached me on the porch, I asked him, "Why did you do that?"

"I paid twenty-five dollars for that horse to help plow our fields. He has to learn," he said, offering no apology or remorse. He then sat on the porch steps in total exhaustion and bathed in sweat.

The following day, he dressed Charley's wounds in some concoction of axle grease and turpentine. Charley recovered over time, but he never pulled a plow. I got some satisfaction from the fact that Charley showed a more granite resolve than John Billy and that there was at least one animal in this world that he could not intimidate.

Jane bought the farm, so to speak, just as John Billy and the boys were finishing up the spring planting. Jane was pulling the seed sled back to the barn at the end of the day. Jody was riding her, as he often did going to and from the fields. Jane stumbled crossing a drain ditch separating the field just behind the house and our yard. She fell flat broadside on the edge of the yard near the black walnut tree and pinned Jody's leg under her ribs and belly. I was preparing supper and heard his screams. My first thought was a snakebite or wasp sting. I hustled out the back door to find Jody snugly bound to the underside of our dead mule. It looked as if he were riding her with both of his legs still astride her body, but her legs were extended to the side and quivering as she drew her final breath.

Johnny appeared on the scene shortly after I arrived. The two of us were able to dislodge Jody from the under-belly of Jane by placing our feet on the mule's backbone and each pulling on his arms. Jody even helped by pushing with his free leg. Jody popped out from under Jane's hold absent his clodhoppers. Johnny waggled under the mule to rescue Jody's dislodged boot.

He pulled out a slab of leather that looked like an overcooked flapjack. Jody's wince became a grin and then full laughter. The three of us, when John Billy drew up with Red, were sitting cross legged, Indian-style, around our late Jane's dead body. We were braying like mules.

Notwithstanding the grind of farm life and the push for an intense work ethic coming from John Billy, my children, especially the boys, were living the carefree, bucolic lifestyle of farm urchins. The atmosphere was one of lark and revelry, which brought me either to tears or to titters.

Weekdays were glutted with school and chores, leaving little time for any adventurous inspirations, but the weekends, especially Sundays, afforded time for folly and foolery.

John Billy was still a two-packs-a-day unfiltered Camel smoker, but he forbade the boys from taking up the practice. We suspected they were exploring the vile habit by using rabbit tobacco. All boys do. Miss Sarah, a snuff user herself, said there was no harm in smoking rabbit tobacco and that the Indian tribes used a concoction of it to cure all sorts of ills.

Sunday was a day of repentance and reconnaissance for my two older boys. One Sunday, after church, Johnny and Joseph were off on one of their usual post-sermon scouting missions. They had one hundred acres to prospect on and around the farm. If the weather permitted, Slick Rock Creek was more often than not on the docket. The wild plum orchard and a very productive persimmon tree on the bottom-land near the creek were must visits when in season.

I was used to the boys exploring their surroundings. On Sullivan's Island they were out most every day from after breakfast to noon, and they were off again after lunch until suppertime. Life on the island was idyllic, with sun and sand and pirate exploring and fishing—lots of fishing. In Mount Pleasant the escapades were dissimilar to those on the island but no less exhilarating. The boys had matured into sports and less into pirates, but fishing was still an anchor for them. Bicycles had replaced their rambling feet as the preferred manner of transportation.

On the Georgia farm it was different for them yet again. They were back to their feet for adventure. They had their bikes, but the two wheels were useless in the pathless woods and seeded fields. The pirates of Sullivan's Island were now replaced by army men, cowboys and Indians, and a one-hundred-acre game of hide-and-seek, or as they called it, hide-and-seek-and-destroy. They used any manner of weaponry. Pine cones, dirt clods, walnuts, and maypops were the weapons of choice, but they were not above using homemade arrows and Daisy Red Ryder BB guns with a strict rule of not shooting above the armpits. I had to rule out the walnuts because the juice was staining their clothes and fingers.

So the boys were off after church. I didn't expect to see them until suppertime. My two girls spent most Sunday afternoons piddling around the farmhouse with me, and Robert was tagging along with John Billy, who was forever checking his vegetable garden, or inspecting the corn or cotton, or checking to see if the watermelons had blossomed. Robert and John Billy first stopped at the barn to pick up a hoe that John Billy used to stave off any stray weeds that might hazard an appearance in his venerated garden.

As he and Robert approached the barn, they both heard a tittering conversation coming from the side of the barn. John Billy hushed Robert with a finger to his lips as they eased closer to the spirited discussion.

"You try it first," he heard Jody say.

"No, you light yours first," replied Johnny.

"It was your idea," coaxed Jody.

"OK, I'll light them, and then we will do it at the same time," Johnny replied.

John Billy gave them several more minutes of giggling before he turned the corner to find them leaning against the side of the barn in full pull, dragging on their smokes.

"What's going on here?" John Billy shouted.

Jody was in mid-inhale and said nothing. Johnny, whose lips were pursed to exhale as he had seen his daddy do so many times, sucked in air and smoke to the deep recesses of his lungs. He went into a panic, expelling smoke, phlegm and spit. He could not speak, but Jody, who could no longer hold his breath, let out a smoky, but ever-honest reply: "We're smoking."

"Where did you get the cigarettes?" John Billy asked.

"We took two from your pack after church," said Jody, who could be nothing less than honest.

"You stole cigarettes from me?"

"Yes sir," Jody said.

"Johnny, what do you have to say for yourself?" his daddy asked.

"Achgggh, achgggh, achgggh," Johnny wheezed.

I was surprised to see John Billy and the boys back so early. He sent the boys to their room as soon as they entered the house. John Billy told me all about what had happened.

"What did you do?" I asked.

"My first thought was to spank them, but heck, I had my first cigarette when I was younger than Jody. Then I thought I would make them smoke all the cigarettes I had in the pack I was carrying. That would stop any egg-sucking dog. But hey, those things are twenty-five cents a pack, and that would be punishing me. So I gave then one month of restriction. They aren't allowed to go past the barn or the outhouse unless it is to go to one of the fields for work."

Listening intently to his logic of punishment and thinking to myself how ironic it was for a lifetime smoker to punish his boys for mimicking his behavior, I lit up one of his Camels, and I asked him with a wise-cracking tone, "Can I go past the barn and outhouse?"

"No, but you never go past the barn or outhouse anyway."

"Oh," I said. "I was just wondering if I was being punished too."

The boys were very creative with occupying their spare time within the confines of the barn and the privy. They found mule shoes and horseshoes of various sizes strewn about the barn area. They spent half a day building a horseshoe pit. The pitching game became their saving grace from endless boredom.

They cut and fashioned fishing poles from the cane growth by the outhouse. Charley, by this time, was almost healed. So naturally, he gave up his pasturing time to provide rides for all my children. The children even tried to get me to mount our pony, but I could only see myself falling to the fate of Jane and Jody.

The boys were on their final weekend of confinement and as usual were playing a contested game of horseshoes. Just as Jody dislodged a game-winning leaner that Johnny had tossed, a ruckus busted loose in the barn. Our young beagles were on to something. I had learned in a short time that beagles were a special breed of dog, unlike the bird dog. Bird dogs are unstable spastics and overly skittish. They are no fun to be around. However, the beagles are friendly and even tempered. They are happy and loyal. Most of all they are family focused. Their only fault, if I had to assign one, is that they can become single minded when on the hunt.

Beagles have a most unlimited vocabulary. They can go from grunts to whines to howls in one sentence. If they need your attention, it's an annoyingly repeated yelp. If they are resting, it's a whispered sigh. But it is when they are on the hunt that they become the most expressive. In the pack they yodel, and when they're excited, their phrasing becomes the sound of screeching tires, of exotic war whoops and echoes of banshee screams.

It was the echoes of banshee screams that drew our attention to the barn. Sarah and I were nestled on the porch. Sarah was watching Robert and Darlene play in the yard, and I was reading from the book of Ecclesiastes while the boys disputed horseshoe distances from the stake. At the racket, Johnny and Jody sprinted to the barn to investigate while I gathered my kids like a hen with biddies.

I heard Johnny say, "They've jumped something in the barn."

Then I heard Jody join in with the screaming beagles. "It's rats," Johnny yelled, but he could barely be heard above the clamor of Jody and the dogs.

"One just ran over Jody's foot," Johnny yelled, giving me the details of the clamor in the barn.

It looked as if a circus had set up in front of our barn. Dogs were in and out. Dog tails and butts were gyrating to and fro with one-minded excitement. Eventually, the beagles corralled the rats behind the slatted barn door. Johnny and Jody followed the beagles, each wielding a lance like pitchfork. The dogs kept their resolve. There was no escaping for the rats. Systematically, the Knights of Farmdom—Sir Jody, the Little Red Dragon Slayer and Sir John the Mule Tamer—slew the fire-breathing rodents. In all, seventeen rats were slain. What Jody and Johnny didn't kill, the beagles destroyed with a single bite to the scruff of the neck.

John Billy had been visiting his ma and pa. When he returned, the boys proudly displayed their quarry tied to the somewhat bloody barn door.

"We need a cat," he said, missing the point that the boys had had a chivalrous time doing knightly deeds against the black dragons.

The very mention of a cat sent shudders up my spine. I had an enormous fear of cats. They were the embodiment of evil—cunning, sneaky, shrewd. I would rather sleep in a pit of copperheads than have a cat brush my leg.

"There will be no cats here," I stated rather emphatically.

"OK, we'll just have to find a rat snake," John Billy said.

The Knights of Farmdom had their newly assigned quest—a crusade to find the Serpent of Barns.

Chapter 24

Farm Failures and Wrestling Fans

John Billy was not one to embrace a dollar too tightly. Spending, especially on credit, appealed to him. He was ever the optimist that money would find its way to his door, and he was not about to save it for a rainy day. With Jane gone and Charley refusing to be harnessed for plowing, he invested in a used Massey Ferguson tractor. He felt the tractor would do the work of several men, boys, and mules. His thinking was sound, but his pocketbook was unreliable. We were still dining on pork, chickens, eggs, and cow's milk with a mix of early greens. Our table began to flourish as the spring and summer vegetables began to come in, but income from the farm had not flourished at all and would not be realized until late summer. We were hanging on by the skin of our teeth.

John Billy, through a cousin-in-law grapevine connection, heard that the Lockheed Aircraft Corporation in Marietta, Georgia, was hiring security personnel. The cousin-in-law had been hired on as a fireman and urged John Billy to do the same. Lockheed had won a government contract in the summer of 1951 to build the C-130 transport plane. There was big government money to be spent. They needed workers and were willing to pay.

I asked John Billy, "How are you going to work a full-time job in Marietta and run this farm at the same time?"

He had it all planned. "The boys can take care of things until I get home, and we can work Saturdays and Sundays. The tractor is going to cut my work by half."

"How far is it from Villa Rica to Marietta?" I asked.

"About thirty or thirty-five miles. I think I will be able to car pool," he said.

"It's gonna take you an hour each way when you stop for carpoolers. How many hours of daylight do you think you are going to have to work in those fields?" I asked, pressing the point.

"I'll be home by four, and besides, the tractor has lights, you know," he said. And I knew that the "you know" ended the conversation.

John Billy returned from his job interview with his good news.

"I got the job. Start Monday. I'll be working third shift, Monday through Friday," he said.

"What's third shift?" I asked, knowing it wasn't nine to five.

"Eleven to seven," he said.

"Seven? Why, you won't be home 'till after dark. How are you—"

He cut me off. "Not seven at night, seven in the morning," he said. "It's the graveyard shift."

"You mean to tell me that you will be leaving here at nine at night and coming back in the morning at eight? Have you lost your mind? How am I supposed to stay out here by myself? What if one of the kids gets sick?"

"You will be OK. The boys are big enough to take care of things," he reasoned, more to himself than to me.

"John Billy, we only have one car and it wouldn't matter if we had another—I can't drive, and the boys don't have a permit to drive. What am I supposed to do, pile up my five kids on your Massey Ferguson and have Johnny drive to the Villa Rica hospital?" I argued, but I knew it was pointless.

His reasoning continued:" The graveyard shift pays more, and I will be home early enough to have a full day of sunshine to work the farm. It's perfect."

"Yeah, perfect for you," I said. I knew those had to be my final words before he became angry.

Well, it was not perfect. Cotton was a labor-intensive commodity. As the months passed, the drudgery and grind of chopping cotton, poisoning boll weevils, and picking cotton began to take their toll on John Billy. Along with the cotton grind, there were the corn, peanuts, and watermelons, that also needed cultivating.

The work was never ending, and John Billy was scarcely holding on with four hours of sleep each night. The signs came slowly at first. I noticed that he was eating less. His excuse was that he was getting indigestion and all he needed was a little baking soda to help him burp. He began to take baking soda after every meal. He began to forget things, simple things, like putting Red in her stall or setting his alarm. His trips to the outhouse became more frequent and routine—meal, baking soda, need to hit the privy. All of this was followed by the headaches— menacing headaches.

They came on about noon and intensified as the day progressed. With the headaches, sleep became even more elusive. He tried to go to bed earlier, but the insomnia would not allow his brain to settle.

For me and the kids, the mood swings were intolerable. He was more demanding on the boys. The after-church excursions came to an abrupt halt. Poor Sarah, who was my equal with the house chores and meals, was harangued daily about the need to help me more. Even the little ones, Robert and Darlene, were railed at for not helping out more.

I asked John Billy, "Is it worth your health to continue trying to run this wretched farm?"

His answer did not address his health. He tried to explain to me how it would be worth it once the money came in. "We have about fifty acres in cotton. That should bring in about $3,500, and with the watermelons and peanuts and sweet potatoes and corn, we should see about $5,000."

I knew he was padding his numbers, but I asked anyway, "What about the costs? You have seed, fertilizer, cotton poison, feed for Red and Charley, and the cow and the chickens. You have a payment on the tractor. You have kids to feed."

We had never discussed the financial arrangement that he and Mr. Bailey had concerning the farm. "And what about your daddy's cut? How much does he get for his tenant's fee?"

"We will still see a profit, I think. We will do no less than break even. I am going to get daddy to sell me the place. Then we can realize more of the profit."

"Sell you the place? What are you going to use for money? We don't have enough to buy the kids Shredded Wheat for breakfast, and you are going to buy this farm? And speaking of our kids, they never put in for this. They were quite content romping in the sands of Sullivan's Island, before you dragged us to this god-forsaken place. You are falling apart. You can't go on. You are going to fall out on that tractor and die in your precious cotton fields," I said, knowing I was overstepping my bounds.

Very gradually John Billy's health began to improve as the growing and harvesting season stalled toward its conclusion. The headaches were less severe, and the trips to the outhouse were less urgent, and sleep returned, though still only four or five hours each night.

The change in John Billy's pocket was burning. He purchased a used 1950 Ford on credit and splurged by ordering a television set, also on credit. The children knew about but had never seen a television. John Billy and I had seen a television in Rich's Department Store in Atlanta on one of our Christmas-present-buying treks to downtown Atlanta, but it never occurred to me that we would one day purchase one.

Each afternoon the kids, coming home from school, would look from the school bus window to our rooftop to see if the antenna had been installed. It took several days, but directly the television was delivered and installed.

Programing was spotty, to say the least. As I look back years later, all the programs in those early years just seem to run together in my mind. We picked up two stations out of Atlanta, WAGA and WSB. The only clear thing on our TV was the Indian-head test pattern, and it seemed to dominate the screen the majority of the time. I do recall a daytime show called TV Ranch. It was a hillbilly music show. It was on that show that I first saw Brenda Lee.

Robert and Darlene fell in love with Miss Frances of *Ding Dong School* fame. Ding Dong School was the 1950s version of *Mr. Rogers' Neighborhood* and *Sesame Street*. Fred Rogers and Big Bird had nothing on Miss Frances. She taught everything from art to science. Robert's most proud accomplishment was when he followed Miss Frances's directions for growing a sweet potato in a glass mason jar.

The most enjoyable option of our early TV programming was wrestling. It was a family affair. In the summer, with the heat, we would place the TV in a bed room window, facing our front porch. With John Billy off to Lockheed, the rest of the family, with swatters in hand, would retreat to the front porch. A fan was used to blow the hot Georgia air across our sweating bodies, and swatters were used to fight the relentless fight against mosquitos, flies, gnats, or whatever hard-crusted flying bug tried to join the wrestlers on the TV screen.

Wrestling had everything. It was drama, comedy, and action. It had midgets, women, masked men, evil Russians, and even more evil Germans. All my children had a favorite wrestler. My favorite was Gorgeous George, a flamboyant Goldielocks that the rest of the family loved to hate. I found the women wrestlers repulsive, but the Fabulous Moolah drew my attention in a carnival freak show kind of way.

The male wrestlers were massive and athletic and wore the tiniest trunks imaginable. Argentina Rocca was the most entertaining. He wrestled shoeless and was forever doing cartwheels in the ring, and he would slap his opponent in the face with his feet. It was simply great family entertainment.

John Billy was quick to realize that the television was counterproductive to his farm, and it presented a dilemma he did not anticipate. TV was a visual outlet, and as the name suggests, television was meant to be seen, and for it be seen by a body, that body had to be stationary, and more often than not, seated—thus the pickle for John Billy. He didn't cotton to anyone being seated during daylight hours unless it was him on his Massey-Ferguson or the outhouse two-seater.

Promptly, there developed implicit rules for TV viewing on the Bailey farm. Rule 1: If John Billy was awake, the TV must remain in the OFF position. Rule 2: If John Billy was awake, he, and only he, could void Rule 1 by turning the TV to the ON position. Rule 3: No child under the age of twenty-one was to have access to the TV until all work was complete.

In time, John Billy's strict control of the television relented as more entertaining shows began to appear in those early years of TV. We, as a family, were allowed more access, especially during the wintry months, but the control of what we watched was still in his hands. No one complained, though. The novelty of television was such that we would have watched ice melt as long as Red Skelton tried to make it funny.

The worry of work to be done versus television viewing was short lived. John Billy felt he needed to own the farm to realize its full financial prospects. Of course, he had no money to purchase the farm from his pa, but he was working the farm with the promise that someday it would be his. Unfortunately, John Billy and his pa had never developed any improvement in their ability to communicate. Neither had a clear idea of the specifics of this farm. I think Mr. Bailey saw a tenant relationship with John Billy and his sons, while John Billy had in mind a lease-to-own expectation. They never had talked specifics and certainly had no contract. The only thing they had in writing was the letters they had exchanged when we were in Charleston, and even those were vague.

The conversation between Mr. Bailey and John Billy over the future of the farm was about as productive as the conversation John Billy had with our horse Charley over the need for him to help with the plowing chores. Both Mr. Bailey and John Billy were as stubborn as the red mule that came with the farm. Once minds were set, there was little likelihood of reason coming from either side. Any glimmer of hope that we would be able to purchase the farm from Mr. Bailey ended with the 1952 presidential election. Mr. Bailey, a devout Democrat, was convinced that the Republicans, who had gained control of the White House and both houses of Congress, would destroy farmers, small business, and the American way of life. He told John Billy that he was doing him a huge favor by not selling him the farm. "With Republicans in power, you would lose the farm in two years," he offered as his final word on the matter.

Chapter 25

On the Road Again

We finished out the harvest season that year. The price of cotton dropped another $2.50 per pound, leaving us with less farm income than the year before. The extra acre of watermelons helped somewhat to close the gap, but we still had less to show for our work than the first year.

John Billy's Lockheed job afforded him the luxury to be able to say to his pa that he was abandoning the life of a floundering farmer. Oddly enough, Mr. Bailey did not protest. He saw that the farm was not going to turn a profit, or at least not enough profit to warrant our continuing in farming futility.

Mr. Bailey had a knack for turning a profit with the buying and selling of farm-land. His farm that we lived on had the one hundred acres, a livable main house, and two somewhat livable tenant houses. Within the year of our leaving, he sold the old place for $4500, which gave him a piddling profit and the good riddance of a money-sucking vacuum of Georgia red clay.

From what we understood, the man who purchased the home-place rented out the three homes and sold the timber to recover his investment in the first year.

As was his manner, John Billy avoided any consultation with me on the selection of our new home. With the kids being established in the Villa Rica school system, he decided that we would remain in Villa Rica. I doubt he ever considered returning to Charleston since he wouldn't be able to find a better job than his fireman's position at Lockheed, and too, I no longer had a link to the tidewater except for my pompous aunts and uncles and their spawn.

John Billy came in late one Friday early that fall with his good tidings.

"I have found us a place. It's just south of town on Sunset Boulevard. It's close enough to the school for the kids to walk, and there is enough room in the back for me to have a garden."

I had lived on Station 26 1/2 on Sullivan's Island, South Carolina, and RFD Route #1 in Villa Rica, Georgia. Sunset Boulevard resonated as a hearth of gentility and respect.

"Oh really? You have already found us a place? When can I go see it?" I asked.

"We are moving in tomorrow morning. You can see it then. I have a couple of firemen coming over to help me and the boys. You need to start packing up things from the kitchen," he said as he headed to the outhouse. "I'll tell you more about it while we are packing."

We discussed nothing about the home on Sunset Boulevard as we packed. John Billy and the boys moved all the heavy pieces of furniture to the back porch so they could easily be loaded when his firemen friends came the next morning. Sarah and I packed up the kitchen. By bedtime we were all too tired to discuss the eminence of our estate on Sunset Boulevard.

As my suspicions warranted, the house on Sunset Boulevard was not a boost to our standard of living. The house was a third the size of our farm house and half the size of our home on Sullivan's Island. The only upgrade was that we didn't have to haul our heat and water from a woodpile or well.

Stepping in the front door, I almost turned and hotfooted it back to the farm. There were no walls in the house to separate the rooms. On either side of the living room were four-foot-high counter stands that functioned as privacy barriers to two bedrooms. The kitchen was no more than an extension of the living room, with only a bed-sheet to partition it off from the gaping open space of the entire house. Left of the kitchen was a small bathroom with a tub, a sink, and a toilet. The turnaround space was so small that one could bathe, shave, and poop all at the same time.

I said to John Billy, "There are only two bedrooms. Where are the boys going to sleep?"

"Follow me," he said.

He took me out the back door onto a small stoop. Off to the left of the stoop was a door to an add-on room.

"They can sleep in there. There is enough room for a bed and maybe a dresser if we put it in the corner," he said as if he had it all figured out.

"Where is the heater?" I asked. "They will freeze. And there are no windows. They will roast in the summer."

"I never had heat in my bedrooms growing up. An extra quilt will work fine. Besides, all three will be in the same bed. There will be plenty of heat from their bodies, and having no windows will keep the flies out in the summer."

He had it all figured out.

"You mean to tell me that my boys are going to have to go outside every night to go to their bedroom?" I asked with as much sarcasm as I could muster.

John Billy simply laughed. "They will adjust," he said.

"They may adjust, but I won't," I snapped under my breathe.

John Billy, being like his daddy, could never settle in one place. He was always seeking to elevate our housing standard—and I suppose, his own personal standing. Our settlement on the pretentious, Hollywood-masquerading Sunset Boulevard was short lived.

Memories there are spotty and fragmented. There was the rat terrier, Mitsy, who was forever bringing us live baby rabbits from the field beyond the sun-baked red clay of Sunset Boulevard that fronted our house. It was on that same unpaved road that the maternal Mitsy and an orphaned rabbit rescue met their destiny when they were struck by a routed taxi from the Villa Rica Cab Company.

There is the memory of the worst beating John Billy delivered to any of our children. He was infrequent with his need for spankings, as a stern look or strong word of admonishment usually took care to address any youthful transgression. The rare spankings were of the nature of hand swats on the bottom while offering a timely cadence of behavioral enlightenment to match each smack—nothing harmful, but very effective. I, myself, was not apologetic when I had to cuff one of my cubs, though the intensity was much less severe and was most often followed by a squeeze of forgiveness. My memories of the nuns at the orphanage in Charleston and my recollections of my own pa's inebriated fits of anger precluded me from any heavy-handed discipline. This, of course, was not John Billy's path to punishment. Where I rejected the angered wrath of my disciplinarians, John Billy, though not consciously, followed in his pa's footsteps. A childish peccadillo begat anger; anger begat punishment; uncontrolled anger begat unbridled reprisal.

The walk to or from the Villa Rica school from our home on Sunset Boulevard was just under a mile. Unlike in the old joke of walking to and from school up hill in both directions, the walk to school was downhill and the walk home was uphill, as Sunset Boulevard crested along a high plateau just south of town. One of my older kids was assigned to walk with Robert, who was now a first grader at the school. On the day of the incident that sparked the beating, Sarah was assigned the babysitting task of escorting Robert safely home. Unlike Johnny or Jody, Sarah took her responsibility more seriously and expected Robert to keep up with her every step. Just as the two of them reached the intersection of South Dogwood and the Carrollton Highway, it began to rain. With a half mile to go, Sarah began to urge Robert to pick up his pace. He lagged behind, and as the rain picked up, she became more demanding. She did not want to get drenched, and Robert enjoyed her frustration. Tired of pleading, Sarah began to scream at Robert, and moved forcibly to get him to follow her by yanking on his ear. The more he resisted, the harder she pulled on his ear and the louder she shrieked.

A passing neighbor, bemused at the battling hellions on Highway 61, stopped to offer assistance. The neighbor coaxed them to accept a ride home. Reluctantly, Sarah and Robert accepted her offer, as the rain showed no signs of letting up, and Sarah wasn't sure she would be able to get Robert home without removing his ear.

John Billy, because of his night shift work at Lockheed, was just arising from his sleep. In fact, it was the neighbor who awakened him with her ceaseless pounding on the front door. As soon as I answered the door, she began an arresting harangue of confusion. I picked up on the rain, the screams, and the ear pulling but had no idea she was alluding to my kids, who were still in the back seat of her vehicle.

John Billy, hearing her ruckus, came to the door.

"Hello, Mrs. Newell. What in the world is going on? Why are you so upset?"

Mrs. Newell took a deep breath, relaxed, and told her story of seeing Robert and Sarah down on the highway having a conniption fit. She didn't stay relaxed for long. As she painted her rendering of the events on Highway 61, her commentary became more embellished. She near duplicated Sarah's screams, and I expected at any moment she would start pulling on John Billy's ear.

John Billy commended Mrs. Newell for being a good neighbor and for watching out for his kids. He promised that she would never have to lay eyes on his kids behaving in such a manner again.

"If you will send the kids in from your car, I will take care of this immediately," he said to her.

Sarah and Robert avoided eye contact with Mrs. Newell as they passed her in the driveway. She stared them down like a barn owl musing over a rat.

My notion was that the old biddy should mind her own business. There was no need for her to get a bee in her bloomers over two young kids having a squabble in the rain. They'd work it out eventually. However, I could tell that John Billy did not share my judgment on the situation. As soon as Sarah and Robert entered the front door, he began to remove his belt. Both kids knew what was coming to them.

John Billy folded his belt, holding the buckle and tip at the base of his palm. This gave him a full arm's length and fourteen inches of leather to administer his due punishment. There was no discussion. There was no pleading of the case. There was no bargaining. Punishment was to be swift and severe. John Billy had heard all the evidence he needed from Mrs. Newell.

Sarah, who was still soaked from the rain, was the first to receive her rawhide whipping. John Billy started out controlled but very quickly snapped into an intemperate anger reminiscent of his beating of our horse Charley. Sarah screamed to the high heavens, and luckily for her there was another offering cowering on the sofa.

He loosed Sarah's arm, and she came running to me. I squirreled her away to her bedroom for fear that he might resolve to make this a circuit from one child to the other. That, and the fact that I had no appetite for watching him violate another of my kids. But since our house had no walls, only four-foot divisions, I could see the blows coming down and could hear Robert's caterwauling pleas and promises that he would never do it again.

When he finished, John Billy sent Robert outside to his bedroom, and he himself went back to our bedroom, sat on the bed, and smoked a Camel.

It was Sarah's misfortune to have been wearing a dress. Her legs, bottom, and back were striped with one-inch near-bleeding welts—fifteen in all. I dressed her wounds with ointment, brought her back down from howling lamentations to breath-catching snot dribbles, and left her with her baby sister so that I could check on Robert.

Johnny and Jody, by this time, had come home from school. As was their habit, they went straight to their room, where they found Robert mortified and confused. By the time I got to him, they had him calm and composed. When I dropped his pants to apply ointment, both Johnny and Jody drew back.

"What happened?" Jody asked.

I told them the story about the screaming match on Highway 61, and the ear pulling, and about Mrs. Newell bringing them home, and about her antics on the porch.

"He didn't need to do that," Johnny said as he pulled Robert down on the bed trying to pin him for a wrestler's three count. Jody, the referee, counted, "one, two, th—" But just before he got to three, Johnny allowed Robert to flip him off the bed.

I have never been able to understand the use of fear and intimidation when leveled at children, or animals for that matter, as a means of coercion to bring about a change in behavior. I saw it all my life from the heartless nuns at the orphanage to my pa's browbeating me and Sis to the stories John Billy told about his pa. It seems to me that a charitable proffering of human kindness would have a more lasting outcome and would remove for all concerned the dread of a recurrence of an outburst.

I didn't speak to John Billy for the balance of the evening, or even give him a kiss when he left for work. He said not a word to Sarah or Robert, and at supper, the mealtime was as silent as kudzu growing on a Georgia pine.

The following morning John Billy came home from work and acted as if nothing had happened. He did this often. He would have his blowup, take a time-out, and be back to his normal self within hours. Yet he never chewed over the past. Perhaps it was because he was embarrassed at his behavior. Perhaps it was because he didn't want to face those demons of his uncontrolled behavioral imperfections. Or perhaps it was because he was resentful of seeing his pa in himself.

My frustration with John Billy was that he was not capable of seeing that the children had a subsurface fear of him. I have no doubt that he loved our children, and they loved him as well, but their fearfulness was beginning to build up an abyss of separation that might one day mirror the relationship he had with his own pa.

But, I knew there was no purpose in trying to talk reason with him. He was blind to the truth that he could be wrong. He was firmly convinced that children lacked self-control and needed strict reminders. He was convinced the children must have unwavering respect for all authority, be it for a teacher, for an adult neighbor, or most especially for him. He knew that children were selfish and willful and would engage in belligerent behavior that could be dangerous to themselves and to others. His solution was pure and simple—use the firm hand or belt, if necessary, as a constant reminder to amend those natural deficiencies. He was an Old Testament parent following the guide of Proverbs: "Folly is bound up in the heart of a child, but the rod of discipline drives it far from him," or "Do not withhold discipline from a child; if you strike him with a rod, he will not die."

I, on the other hand, had seen this approach all my life from adults who bullied kids to parents who had no compassion for their children. I took a New Testament approach with my children: "For God gave us a spirit not of fear but of power and love and self-control." Perhaps the conjoined testaments of childrearing served a purpose.

Chapter 26

On the Road Again—Sing the Same Old Song

I think from the moment we set foot in that shell of a box on Sunset Boulevard, John Billy was prospecting Villa Rica for an upgrade in housing. All three boys kept a constant cold that winter from sleeping outside in a room with no ventilation and no heat. Since John Billy needed his sleep during the day, the kids were imprisoned in a world of silence from the time they got home from school until the time that John Billy awakened for supper. A change was sorely needed.

In the mid-fifties Villa Rica was small-town America. Housing opportunities were wanting. There were a few pocketed neighborhoods, each with its own enclave of doctors, businessmen, or mill owners. Those quarters on the south side of the tracks were not within our means, being reserved for the more moneyed of Villa Rica's villagers. East and west of Villa Rica along Highway 78, the Bankhead Highway, was a scattering of homes with acreage increasing with distance from down-town. Again, those homes were out of our price range, and the last thing we needed was a place with acreage because John Billy would have been right back to farming. North of the tracks was the village of Fullerville, an inclusive mill town that had seen better days. Most houses there were allocated to the mill workers.

Through church connections, John Billy got wind of a lady whose husband had recently passed. She had a rental she was wanting to sell. Her house was on the fringe of Villa Rica and Fullerville. It was mill town housing without the amenities. It was downtown without the highway. Most importantly, it wasn't the cocoon on Sunset Boulevard.

John Billy offered to take me to see the house before he made his offer to buy it.

"Does it have interior walls?" I asked.

"Yes," he laughed.

"Do the boys get to sleep indoors?"

"Yes, and they each can have their own bed," he added.

"I'll take it, sight unseen."

We did, however, take a tour before moving in. The house was located on Walker Street. It was less than a mile walk from our new neighborhood to downtown Villa Rica, the Villa Rica school, the EZ Shoppe food store, and a soon-to-be-built hospital. Most every home within rock-throwing distance and had children of varying ages and sizes, giving my kids friendships and playmates. Isolated in the midst of the neighborhood and abutted next to our lot was a family-run hosiery mill which delivered a constant twenty-four-hour mechanical drone.

The house itself was a cutout copy of most mill houses of that time. The floor plan layout was four evenly sized rooms. There was a living room on the front side and a bedroom, also on the front. Each had its own separate entrance. The two rooms on the back side were another bedroom and a kitchen. The kitchen and back bedroom were bisected by a single bathroom with only a tub and toilet.

The girls were assigned the back bedroom. Leading from their bedroom was a narrow set of stairs to the attic. The attic had been converted into two half pentagon-shaped rooms with little headroom except at the apex of the ceiling.

In the living room, there was a single gas heater that had been fitted into an old fireplace box. That was the lone heat source for the house, unless one counted the kitchen stove, which we did count on cold mornings when the kids were getting dressed for school. It took a while for the room to heat up on cold mornings, so the kids had to gather around the gas stove or the oven to dress for school. They would drape clothing on a chair or magazine rack near the heat to warm before putting it on, and they were constantly rotating from front to back to keep a steady heat across their bodies until they could don the fully toasted garments. On many a morning, the living room smelled of scorched school apparel. The worst was when Robert would leave his Keds too close to the flame. For hours the house smelled of burnt canvas and rubber. I think we were very fortunate that one of the kids didn't burn the house down.

Even with their faults and limitations, the house and neighborhood on Walker Street were an upgrade from the box on Sunset Boulevard. The convenience to town and having people in the neighborhood were the biggest pluses. Yet I was reminded very quickly that there was a peculiarity of personalities with all small towns. That fact was even more glaring in Villa Rica. I saw it in Mount Pleasant and I saw it on Sullivan's Island. Heck, my own ma was one of the oddities on the island, walking the beaches talking to herself or writing the president on grocery sacks from the Piggly Wiggly.

It seems that town characters always have a similar story. For the females it is often the trauma of a romance gone bad or the loss of a loved one. She is emotionally destroyed by her experience, and her life's melodrama plays out in front of the towns-folk.

Sybil, or "Sybil the Uncivil" the town called her, was one such wayfarer in Villa Rica. Syble lived in a kudzu-covered farmhouse that had seen better days. Her place was two miles north of town. She made the walk to town daily with no apparent aim other than to walk aimlessly. Walker Street was on her route. The kids always knew when she was passing because the Walker Street dogs greeted Sybil with snarls, barks, and covert charges. My kids would gather at the front windows to watch Sybil and the mongrels.

Sybil always dressed in black—black low-heeled pumps, black stockings with snaked seams that suggested she had no mirror in which she could check alignment, a long-sleeve-buttoned-up-to-the-neck A-line dress, and a black funeral hat. She accessorized with black gloves and a large black purse. In her purse she carried a variety of knives, which she brandished at the attacking dogs.

I tried to engage Sybil whenever she passed our house and to help her rid herself of the gathering hounds. I would meet her at the edge of our driveway with a greeting of "How are you today, Miss Sybil?" Somedays there would be no acknowledgment that I was even present. Some days though talking to herself, she would eyeball me as if she were addressing me. Then there were days when I would see a glint of clarity as she cussed the dogs.

Then there was "Tickle" Pink—Theodore Pinkney, to be more precise. Tickle was an eighteen-year-old freshman at the high school who was more of an errand boy for the coaches there than a student. When he wasn't assisting one coach or another as team manager, depending on the sport in season, Tickle would moonlight as a gofer for the town merchants.

Far from being a scholar, Tickle could not cipher his numbers.

Tickle, what is twenty-five plus twenty-five?" someone would ask.

"Forty-five," Tickle would answer with confidence.

No matter his deficiencies in higher math, Tickle was a master of monetary calculation.

"Tickle, if I gave you twenty-five cents and someone else gave you twenty-five cents, how much money would you have?" That would always be the follow-up question to his first mathematical brainteaser.

Without hesitation, Tickle would answer, "Fifty cents."

Every kid in the Villa Rica school was astounded at Tickle's ability to correctly add or subtract change yet be clueless in basic arithmetic. Tickle was forever baited with rote number crunching, but he never got tired of it. In fact, he seemed to take pride in his ability to make change in his head.

From the moment we moved into the Walker Street home, and as fast as I could say "shrimp and grits," John Billy began to get involved in local politics. It started, I suppose, when he would frequent town, purchasing seed and whatnot for the farm. The local feed store was the gathering place for farmers to discuss crop failures and politics. And although he was losing his hair on the top of his head, he still needed the deliverance of the local barbers to groom the nape and lower the ears. It was here that he was groomed, not only for his thinning hair but also in local political affairs.

His jump start into the Villa Rica political arena began when he became the coach of the local Little League and Babe Ruth League baseball teams. Jody and Robert were both of age to participate in both leagues. He coached for the benefit of his sons, no doubt, but also because of some newfound appetite for civic duty.

He reached out to the town elite for help in donating funds to purchase uniforms and equipment. Hand shaking and a back-patting "thank you for your help with the young boys of Villa Rica" endeared John Billy to the doctors, lawyers, and Indian chiefs of the city.

It seemed his passion for civic duty had no bounds. With five chil-dren in the Villa Rica school system he ran and was selected to head the school's parent teachers association. This led to more hand shaking, name recognition, and more fund raising. The Atlanta-based TV show, *Stars of Tomorrow* with host Freddie Miller, held an audition show at the school auditorium. The PTA held its own minstrel show, and most popular of all was the womanless wedding starring all Villa Rica's most noble nabobs. Each event and fund-raiser acquainted John Billy with the voting public in Villa Rica.

It was after a first and successful season of coaching and his first year as PTA president that he was approached by several businessmen to run for the town council. Elections were held in November, but he already had a jump on his opponent with all his previous glad-handing for the baseball teams and school functions.

John Billy won handily by about one hundred votes in the city elec-tion of 1956.

I, too, went through some personal changes. Villa Rica had its wife beaters, Jezebels, two-timers, degenerates, and delinquents. Some lived in a veiled, shadowy field of silence, but most were the talk of the town. The small-town rumor mill in Villa Rica was more productive than a Fullerville sock factory.

Being a newcomer to town, I was often in the dark about the players, but my neighbors, hair dresser, and Sunday school sisters energetically brought me up to snuff. John Billy brought home enough slander from the barbershop to complement the whispers I had heard from the ladies in town.

I knew who was sleeping with whom. I knew which man was beating his wife and which wife was domineering to her husband. I knew the ladies of the night who were actually ladies of the day who were play-ing while the master was away. I knew the kids twixt twelve and twenty who were hostile and pernicious and from whom I needed to shield my own kids.

This is not to say that Villa Rica was the Peyton Place of west Georgia. I had read the novel just after our move into town. As my town gossipers shared their tales of iniquity, I could see parallels to the Grace Metalious novel. Thinking back on Sullivan's Island, Mount Pleasant and Charleston, I cannot help but think that there is a pulp paperback blistering to be written regarding every small town and neighborhood in America.

There was that seedy side, no doubt, but there was also the principled, the honorable, the right-minded side. Living in town and meeting fresh faces led to a repeated conversation. "How do you do? Glad to meet you!" was followed by "Where do you all go to church? We would love to have you worship with us at . . ."

I was still a Catholic, but in name only. There was no Catholic church in Villa Rica, nor was there a synagogue or temple. If you weren't Baptist, Methodist or Presbyterian you were out of luck in town. On the outskirts you could find a Holiness Church or Church of Christ or even Mr. Bailey's foot-washing Hard-Shells. Since the Villa Rica First Baptist was only a quarter of a mile from our doorstep and John Billy was somewhat of a Baptist, we chose that route for our family's salvation and deliverance.

The saving of my soul and the souls of my children became the collective commission of the Villa Rica First Baptist Church. The church members were tenacious. Four of my five kids were in different Sunday school classes, as Johnny and Jody were close enough in age to warrant being classmates. They were blitzed from all angles with God's Word.

Part of the strategy to convert the family was the church choir. It mattered not that anyone could sing as long as the person could make a joyful noise. Johnny and Jody were in the youth choir, Sarah was in the intermediate choir, and Robert was in the junior choir. Darlene had to wait her turn until she was past singing her only song, "Jesus Loves Me," a song she sang at every opportunity. Her rendition even replaced John Billy's rehearsed prayer before our every meal.

The church doors were opened to the kids most any day of the week. Wednesday was choir practice for the junior choir, Thursday was reserved for the youth choir, and Tuesday was set aside for the intermediate choir. In the summer there was Vacation Bible School. Each holiday—Christmas, Easter, and Thanksgiving—saw a week of singing jubilee and more Baptist indoctrination.

I was reluctant—no, resistant at first. I joined no choirs. I did attend Sunday school classes, Wednesday night prayer services, and regularly sat in the same pew each Sunday morning from 11:00am to noon or 12:23pm, depending on how many were moved by the sermon. All those things I did for my children. For me personally, there was that Catholic guilt that I was forsaking my own religion for John Billy's.

As long as we were isolated on the farm, I had no close friends beyond Miss Sarah and John Billy's sisters, and I only saw them rarely. When I did see them, we didn't talk religion. We talked mostly about children and chicken preparation and, of course, the weather.

My newfound Sunday school friends at Villa Rica First Baptist Church were instrumental in my conversion. I could tell I was their pet project, but I didn't mind. Whereas John Billy and his family rarely talked about religion openly, or anything else for that matter, these ladies talked about nothing else when we were together as a group. They supplied me with verses and passages to read. They gave me bulletins and magazines with the articles they wanted me to read circled in red. And my three closest church friends, Estelle, Dorothy and Louvie quizzed me on everyone.

I had questions and they had answers. I explained that we had liturgy and the Eucharist in the Catholic Church. They clarified for me that the Baptist had something similar.

"We have worship service, which is like mass and we drink the blood and eat the body of Christ about once a month, usually at the Sunday evening service," explained Dorothy.

"Do y'all drink wine and eat the wafer?" I asked.

Estelle broke it down for me. "Oh, Lord no. This is a dry county. We use Welch's grape juice and soda crackers."

"Do y'all drink wine in the Catholic church?" Louvie asked me.

"Yes, sometimes. It depends on the parish. Sometimes it's just the body—that is, the bread. They say if you eat the body, you are getting the blood too."

"What about children? Do they drink wine?" Louvie continued.

"Sometimes, but it's just a sip, or the priest might dip the wafer in the wine. It all depends," I tried to explain.

"They don't see that as a sin, drinking?" asked Dorothy.

"They told me that the sin was drunkenness, not drinking," I answered.

"Lord, around here it's a sin just to snuff the stuff, but you can get beer at the VFW if you want it," said Estelle.

"Well, I don't want it," I laughed.

"No, I didn't mean you. I meant anyone who had a hankering," she said, laughing along with me.

"So why are the Catholic churches so fancy inside?" asked Louvie. "They could use that money they spent on decoration to feed the poor."

"Well, here is what they told me. In the early church, people couldn't read, and besides, there were few Bibles printed, and plus, they spoke in Latin. So the churches used the stained-glass windows, statues, and paintings on the walls and ceilings to tell the Gospel. My ma said that Jesus was about goodness, mercy, and beauty, so the art covered the beauty part. I guess too it gave people a sense of what heaven might be like," I explained as best I could.

"Well now, that makes sense. All we have at the First Baptist is wood and plaster and some colored windows, but let's not tell Preacher Collins. He might raise the tithe," chimed in Dorothy.

My three friends and I met once a week for Bible study. Occasionally, other members of our Sunday school class would be invited, but I think it was for the extra vittles more so than for their mastery of the Bible. I learned that Bible study, like everything the Baptist did, involved food. Not only did I gain religion, I gained an additional fifteen pounds.

Our study group started in Genesis and moved our way toward the Gospels and Paul. We skipped the food laws in Leviticus and Deuteronomy and some of the more violent stuff like Sodom and Gomorrah.

My friends told me that everything was up for discussion. For the parts where there were no explainable answers, my friends had a pat answer: "It was God's will."

"How do you suppose Noah got all those animals and their food on the boat?" I asked.

"It was a godly miracle. You see, God can do anything. All you need is faith the size of a mustard seed and the understanding that He can move mountains," Estelle said, simplifying it for me.

I never understood why anyone would want to move a mountain.

"If Adam and Eve were the first two people, and they had three sons, who did the boys marry?" I asked.

My three prayer partners looked at each other, and then finally Dorothy offered an explanation: "Well, obviously God made them in his image, He just didn't tell about it in the book.

We quickly made our way through the Old Testament. I don't think my friends wanted to ponder too long on how Moses parted the Red Sea, or why the lions didn't eat Daniel, or why God kept killing Philistines.

Mind you, I had not been to church since I got out of the orphanage except for Easter and Christmas or when the kids had some pageant at the church on the island. Once we moved to the Georgia farm, we would make an occasional visit to the Pleasant Grove Baptist Church located on a dirt road east of town near John Billy's folks' house. My knowledge of the Bible was limited except for what the nuns beat into us at the orphanage.

I found the New Testament just as puzzling as the Old.

"How can Jesus be a god, if God said in the commandments that we should have no other gods before him?" I asked.

"Well, Christians believe in the Trinity," Dorothy said.

I don't think any of my friends considered the Catholic Church to be Christian.

"You see, there is God the Father, God the Son—Jesus, and God the Holy Ghost. They are three, but they are one and the same," Dorothy continued.

"Well, I get God and Jesus, father and son, but the Holy Ghost I don't understand," I said.

"It's the spirit of God and Jesus," Louvie added. "God and Jesus are not with us in the flesh, but their presence is with us through the spirit, the Holy Spirit," she explained, and proud of her answer she was.

"So when you tell me that I will know when Jesus speaks to me, it will be through this Holy Spirit?" I asked, thinking that I had made a break through.

"That's correct. You will know. You will feel it," Estelle added.

That summer the Holy Spirit came for a visit. The visit was first sparked by a TV viewing of a Billy Graham crusade back in the spring. Reverend Graham spoke to me, and I suppose the Holy Spirit was there as well. The theme of the Graham sermon was "Is my heart right?" He wanted to know if I had a sinful heart. I didn't think so, because I didn't do or say anything hurtful to anyone, but I did sometimes have angry thoughts toward John Billy.

Graham went on to say that one's mouth might be close to God while the heart was far away. I don't know how close my mouth was to God. I did say a prayer every now and again, usually when John Billy was his ornery self or if the kids were on my last nerve, but I wasn't a regular in the church. He went on to say that pride often gets in the way by keeping us from coming to Christ. I could see that. People don't want to humble themselves to admit weakness or failure.

Some are selfish, he said. People will go to someone else, before they turn to God. I had been getting months of advice from Estelle, Dorothy and Louvie but had not yet turned to Jesus for answers. Maybe I was looking in all the wrong places.

The Reverend Graham told me that I needed to be born again. I had been christened when I was a baby but had been drifting away from the church ever since. Maybe it was the hostile nuns who drove me away, I thought. Reverend Graham asked if I would like for Christ to transform me, to give me a new moral nature, and if I wanted a new creation?

I startled my kids when I shouted from the living room, "Yes, yes, yes!"

The preacher told me to give my life to Christ for a new heart just before telling his audience members, who had filled some baseball stadium, to come forward to receive Christ. As a crowd started forward toward the preacher's podium, I wanted to jump through my fourteen inch RCA screen to join them. I had, indeed, felt a calling. But after all of the cookies, cakes, and casseroles from my meetings with Dorothy, Estelle, and Louvie, there was no way for me to slip through the TV screen to the baseball diamond to answer Billy Graham's summons. I had to wait.

And wait I did. That summer the Villa Rica First Baptist Church held a revival. Dorothy told me that the church leaders would call for a revival when they felt there was a need for one. I guess the Lord had put a bug in Preacher Collins's ear that I was in need of a revival.

The Holy Spirit didn't come to visit me until Friday, the last night of the revival. All week I had watched as others responded to the benediction. I was determined not to join the crowd. All my life I had been a follower, a puppet. I was determined to do this on my own. Neither John Billy nor my three Baptist friends were going to make this call. This was between me and the Holy Trinity.

On Friday night it hit me. I felt overcome with emotion. A voice in my head told me I was ready. I am guessing that was the voice of the Holy Spirit. I moved down to the front of the church, where Preacher Collins was waiting to meet and greet his lost lambs. I didn't know what I was supposed to say to the preacher. I didn't know how to express what I was feeling.

"A voice in my head spoke to me" was the first thing I said to the preacher.

"I am sure it did. That voice has been speaking to me all week. It told me you were coming down. God bless you," said the preacher.

"What do I do now?" I asked.

"Just stand up here with me. Let everyone bask in the glory of Jesus and your new commitment to the Lord," he said.

"Do you want to come over for dinner on Sunday after your sermon?" I asked him.

"I'll be there," he said with a opossum grin on his face.

So there I was, a former Catholic from the white sands of Sullivan's Island, South Carolina, standing next to a red-clay Baptist preacher in Villa Rica Georgia. The journey felt complete, or so I thought.

Chapter 27

Baptism Pool and Exploding Town

Two weeks after my conversion came the hour of my Baptist baptism. For most of my adult life, Pope Pius XII had been my church's spiritual leader. Now, as a Baptist, I was about to become my own spiritual leader. Quite a change, no doubt, but I felt comfortable in my new role.

I had attended a few baptisms when we frequented the little country Pleasant Grove Baptist Church in Villa Rica. Its baptismal pool was a small lake about fifty yards south of the church. After a protracted sermon of almost two hours, the entire flock of Sunday service worshippers sauntered over to the lake to partake in the ceremonial immersion. The dunker and the "dunkees" were veiled in salvaged choir robes that were long past their glory-hallelujah days. As the newfound souls lined the lake's sandy bar, waiting for their moment of divine oneness with Jesus, the congregation and the choir joined in singing "Down to the River to Pray" and "Shall We Gather at the River." The reverend prayed, hand held high to the heavens, making reference to John the Baptist and Jesus. One by one, I witnessed the newborn foundlings of God take their turn in this old-fashioned ritual. As each emerged from the murky holy waters of the Pleasant Grove Baptist Church lake, washed pure of their sins and muddied from foot to forehead, they were met by family and well-wishers.

I often counted my blessings that I was not baptized in that lake. Thirty years living on the Atlantic Ocean, and I still could not swim, and living on the farm, I had garnered a loathing for all things feral and crawly. Who knew what lurked beneath those dark shadowy waters, consecrated or not? Had we remained at that pastoral parish, I doubt I would ever have become a Baptist. Creepy-crawly and spirit cleansing just don't mix.

Compared to the bog and pond scum of the Pleasant Grove Baptist Church lake, the Villa Rica First Baptist Church's baptistery was state-of-the-art. The water had a tint of swimming pool blue reflecting from the painted sides of the bowl. The water was warmed by heating elements planted on either side of the tank, and most importantly, there were steps leading down to the floor of the pool. There was no green algae, no Jesus bugs, and no stench seeping through the godforsaken slime like at the lake's bottom. I was safe and secure from all alarm, or so I thought.

Preacher Collins approached from one set of stairs, and once firmly planted, he offered peace and prayers to the congregation. The waters were at low rib height on the pastor. At five feet with heels, I knew the water would be lapping my neck, and being heeless did nothing to comfort my building apprehension.

Words from the preacher about cleansing my soul or my faith in Christ or my rebirth did little to comfort my fears of the rising waters from the girth of the preacher. I was convinced that the water was now snout deep to this proselytized, unwashed landlubber. My aversion to the deep flooded my head with thoughts of retreat. I longed for the shallow waters of the Pleasant Grove Baptist Church lake, creatures and all.

A smile and the outreached hand of Preacher Collins did little to ease my anxiety. However, a glance out to the fold offered reassurance, especially the beaming faces of Dorothy, Estelle, Louvie, and my five children. I could hear the voice of John Billy behind me with a demanding "Go on!"

I sidled down the steps, the waters deliberately cresting toward my neck. I could picture the floods of Noah washing me far afield from the ark. Then, from the final step to the floor of the pool, I realized that the water was not going to engulf my head. I was safe but oblivious to the the preacher's words. All I remembered of the ritual was the words "in the name of the Father, Son, and Holy Spirit" and the grabbing of my nose just before the dunking.

As Preacher Collins escorted me from the pool toward John Billy, who was waiting with a shell-cluttered beach towel to dry me off, I spied a gargantuan spider lurking in the corner of the baptismal pool. Satan had sent it, I was sure. I stepped back again in retreat. Just as I had been hesitant to descend the steps to the baptismal pool, I wasn't about to ascend those same steps past this guardian of hell. The preacher, sensing my alarm, noticed the black hairy creature and turned me away from the exit and the awaiting towel toward the steps he had descended at the beginning of the ceremony. At the top of the stairs, he said to me, "Do you know what that spider symbolizes? It is a sign that your influential friends have come to help you when you are in deep waters." As we stepped out of the baptismal pool, I was met by Estelle, Dorothy, Louvie, and my five impassioned kids.

After my immersion conversion, I began to notice a change in John Billy. I wasn't sure if, indeed, the change was in him or in how I perceived him. Regardless, he seemed more mellow and less abrasive. He was more even tempered and less harsh with the kids. He was the John Billy we had left at Barbara's graveside in Mount Pleasant.

After a short adjustment to our new home on Walker Street, life was settling back to its conventional routine. John Billy still left our home each night at nine for his night shift hours at Lockheed. Immediately after he departed for Marietta, I would send one of the boys over to the sock mill next door to purchase Coca-Colas. For a quarter we could get three Coca-Colas and a snack. I loved Junior Mints, while the kids settled for splitting a Mars Bar or Three Musketeers.

By 1957 all the kids were in school. Johnny worked part time after school and on weekends at Berry's Pharmacy on Montgomery Street in Villa Rica. Jody did the same as a bagger at the EZ Shoppe across from the new hospital on the Dallas High-way.

My three prayer and Bible studies buddies and I added exercise and diet discussions to our scripture studies to see if we could remove the extra fifteen pounds we had added during the course of saving my soul. We revisited Leviticus and Daniel for motivation and guidance, looking for the do's and don'ts of biblical dining. There was no mention of Coca-Cola or Junior Mints in either Testament, so I was able to justify my nightly food fudge by God's omission of those sugary snacks from the creed. If He didn't want us to partake of Coca-Cola and Junior Mints, He would have had a prophet deliver that message.

We added exercise for good measure in hopes of torching the added fat we had accumulated. We couldn't find Biblical counsel for how to exercise, outside of a few pointers and vague references. Paul told us that the body was a temple of the Holy Spirit within us. Each of our temples hinted of room additions being added. Isaiah provided motivation in saying that God "gives power to the faint, and to him who has no might he increases strength. Even youths shall faint and be weary, and young men shall fall exhausted; but they who wait for the Lord shall renew their strength; they shall mount up with wings like eagles; they shall run and not be weary; they shall walk and not faint."

God, the prophets, Jesus, and the apostles, we discovered, talked often about races and running and winning the prize, but our suspicion was that they were not referring to a Jesse Owens Olympian sprint.

So with no guidance at all, we designed our own workouts. We took a little from our sons' football exercises we had seen on Friday nights—jumping jacks, toe touches, duck walks, bear crawls. We tried push-ups, but none of us could do one. From the girls' basketball team, we picked up jump roping. Our most effective exercise was of our own design—the floor roll. We'd move all furniture to one side and literally roll across the living room floor.

It was during one of these rolling sessions at Louvie's that life in Villa Rica, as we knew it, came to an abrupt halt. Just as I was finishing roll number three and as Dorothy was sliding into position on Louvie's braided cotton area rug for her third roll, the house jolted on its foundation. The tremor was followed, almost simultaneously, by a distant thunderclap. Our immediate integrated fears of earthquakes quickly vanished when Dorothy whipped us back to reality with "What in heaven's name was that?"

Huddling closely, we went to Louvie's front porch. We saw nothing but could sense a hint of a noxious stench. Our unanswerable questions to each other were interrupted by the startling ring of Louvie's phone. It was John Billy.

John Billy, home from work, had already gone to bed when his sleep was interrupted by a call from the mayor. John Billy'a call to me at Louvie's was frantic.

"There has been an explosion downtown," he said. "I am headed there now . . . as soon as I get dressed. Check on the kids. I'll talk to you later. Bye."

Dorothy and Estelle, being the only car drivers in the group, immediately left for home. Louvie and I sat in a puzzled silence until we began to hear the echoes of the fire and police alarms.

At Louvie's suggestion, we decided to walk to town. Each step toward the city was marked with dreaded anticipation. The sounds, the smells, each magnified our uncertainty as to what we were going to find. With that anxiety, our pace grew more hurried and our breathing more labored. Little was shared between the two of us. We each could hear the breathless panting of the other. As we passed the First Baptist Church, we stopped to regain our mettle and to say a prayer for God's deliverance from the unknown we were about to face.

The walk from Louvie's house to town was on an upgrade, but we could see billowing smoke coming from the city's center. At the top of the rise, we began to sense that this was seriously grave. The west entrance to Main Street was blocked by a state patrol vehicle detouring traffic north on Highway 61.

"What on earth has happened?" I asked the patrolman.

"The pharmacy exploded. Gas leak. Looks like most of the town has been leveled. You ladies be careful. We don't know if it could go up again," he said with some panic in his voice.

In another hundred yards we came upon the devastation. We hastened our pace. We could tell immediately that the pharmacy and the adjacent jewelry store were obliterated. The structured outer walls were gone. The building roofs were flush to the ground. Out front in the parking spaces, cars were pancaked into unrecognizable scrap heaps. I was immediately reminded of the hurricane damage I had witnessed on Sullivan's Island.

We settled on the north side of the elevated railroad tracks near the train depot. Men were ripping back and forth, trying to find an opening under the roof to get to the people trapped inside. Indecipherable voices and screams from the rescuers and perhaps the victims added to the chaos.

I looked for John Billy. I found him atop what had been the jewelry store, but he quickly disappeared into the rubble. Other men were tossing brick and blocks and smoking wood pieces. Firemen were attempting to hose down flames and smoking embers and trying to cool the rooftop for the rescuers. John Billy reappeared, pulling a lifeless body from the wreckage. He took a knee until another man came to offer his support in dragging the body to the rear of the buildings to an awaiting ambulance. After some minutes, John Billy reappeared on the roof but again disappeared into the smoldering debris.

All the while funeral home limousines were arriving to help cart the wounded and dead to the hospital. More fire trucks arrived from Douglasville, Temple, and Carrollton. Heavy equipment slowly arrived to help create openings for the rescue workers to more easily enter the hellish inferno.

I saw Johnny and some of the senior football players talking to one of the pharmacists. Before I could get Johnny's attention, all the boys packed into the back of a pickup truck and left the scene. I wove my way through the ever-increasing crowd over to the pharmacist and asked where the boys were going.

"They left school to come help. I received a call from the hospital. They needed help down there, so I sent the boys there. I'm headed that way myself."

"Where you in the pharmacy when it exploded?" I asked him.

"No, ma'am. Thank God. I was supposed to go in at noon. I went over to City Hall to vote before going in to work. Lucky, I guess."

Louvie and I had seen enough, and we needed to get home before our kids arrived from school. Apparently the schools had dismissed the kids after finding out what had happened.

At the corner of Main Street and Highway 61, the state patrolman we had talked to earlier had been replaced by the school's safety patrol students, who were clad in their white belts and identifying badges. They were doing an admirable job of redirecting traffic. Several spoke and asked questions about what was happening downtown. At the Baptist church, Louvie and I made another prayful stop with more particulars for God to consider.

When we arrived home, three of my children were already home, as was Louvie's daughter. Jody and Louvie's two boys had gone to the explosion site. I opened two cans of tomato soup and made sandwiches for us all. Louvie and I told the kids what we had seen. They had lots of questions, most of which we could not answer. I tried to distract the kids by turning on *American Bandstand*. That worked until John Billy came home.

At the fall of the evening, he came in totally exhausted. I had seen him in a similar state when he suffered his physical breakdown when we were on the farm, but this was different. His eyes were a blur, as red as my pa's when he was on a drunk. His face was burned, but not the way it would have been from an island sunburn and wind burn. It was fire-burned almost to the point of a blistering peel. His voice was creaky sounding like Louis Armstrong's on "Up a Lazy River." His shirtsleeve was scorched at the triceps.

"You are burnt," I said. "What happened there?"

"I tripped over something. I couldn't see. I fell on my side. Must have landed on a girder or something. You got any Vaseline?"

I could tell that he wasn't interested in conversation. The kids started to probe with questions, but I hushed them up straight off. He and I went to our bedroom. Sitting on the bed, he began to cry, but the tears were suspended by an unexpected eruption of vomit. The spew covered me, the bedspread, and his pants leg. I had prepared him some fried chicken livers and mashed potatoes, but after seeing his condition,

I simply cleared the bedding and helped him settle. By the time I retrieved the Vaseline jelly from the medicine cabinet for his arm, he was dead to the world. I applied the Vaseline, covered him with a quilt, and left him with the tormented nightmares that were sure to come. I called into Lockheed to tell them he would not be in that night.

Johnny came home about nine. Immediately, he kept me and the other kids raptured with a rapid-fire filibuster of what he had seen at the hospital.

"At first, they had me wheeling people in from the ambulances to the emergency rooms. Some looked dead. Those alive were in horrific pain. Some were in shock, and others just let out a hailstorm of blood-curdling screams. I was scared, but after a few came in, I started to talk to them, trying to get their minds off their pain. I didn't recognize anyone. I kept looking for anyone who might be from the drugstore, but they were all so burnt, and most of the hair on their heads was gone. After most of the bodies came in, the doctors then had me cleaning up some of those who were not severely burned. I stopped counting at twenty, but the bodies kept coming in. After a while nurses from other hospitals and clinics started coming in, so they sent us home."

He went on for what seemed like hours, repeating himself and filling in with new memories of the hell he had witnessed. All the while my thoughts were that if this had happened four hours later, he would have been one of those they were pulling from the wreckage downtown. His shift at the drugstore began as soon as school was let out in the afternoon. I don't think at the time he made that connection—that it could have been him they were dressing at the hospital for burn wounds.

It was Sarah, I think, who asked, "What caused the explosion?"

Johnny repeated what he had heard and told what he knew: "We've been smelling gas for a few days. The gas company came by once, thought they had it fixed, but we could still smell the gas. They said to open the doors and run the fans and the smell would go away in a few days. They were saying at the hospital that the gas company crew came back this morning and were down in the basement working on the leak when the explosion happened. Mr. Hixon and his crew—Mr. Dyer and his son, Johnny, were killed. Mrs. Berry was killed. Ralph Fuller and Ray Tyson were injured. The dentist on the top floor was killed and at least one of his patients."

These were people that I knew. Oscar Hixon was a church member at Pleasant Grove Baptist Church. Margaret Berry was the wife of Bill, the owner of Berry's Pharmacy. My children were classmates with their three kids. Ralph Fuller cut my boys' hair. Ray Tyson worked at the drugstore with Johnny. He was behind the soda fountain when the explosion hit. We later learned that the patient who was killed in the dentist chair was Bobby Roberts. Bobby played midget football with Robert.

Johnny heard that not only did the drug store go up, but a large section of the downtown was also lost. The Five and Dime, the Dress Shop, the florist, and Reeves Jewelry all were damaged beyond recognition. He also heard that they had to call out the Georgia Guard after rumors that there were looters salvaging from the drugstore and jewelry store. I don't know if that was true or not, but when John Billy went back to the explosion site, the Guard was there.

John Billy awoke around two in the morning. He had two cups of coffee but didn't feel like eating anything. I fixed him a sack lunch of boiled eggs and bacon and a banana. He remained hushed. I didn't probe. By two thirty, he was back at the explosion site.

Chapter 28

On the Road Again

My mind could not escape the tragedy that had visited our little town. One moment people were doing what people do in small towns—eating an early lunch at the drug store lunch counter, looking for bargains at the five and dime, buying groceries, voting in a local election, going to school, working to repair a gas leak. I have heard it said that the weeks and months and years go by so quickly but moments last forever. I was certain that that moment at 11:00 a.m. would last for the remainder of my life.

I thought of the story of Esther. People at a time like this needed people—brave people, obedient people, people committed to doing God's work in faith. God places us all where he wants us to be at a time like this. No one in our small town could fathom what God might have in store for each of us, but it was certain, at least to me, that this was a test.

Townspeople gathered in homes and on the few street corners remaining unscarred to share tempers. Party lines kept the phones abuzz with retrospection and introspection. "Why us?" was the great unanswered riddle.

The immediate uncertainties of "Why us?" were followed by an even more dubious "What do we do now?" Because John Billy was on the city council, he was involved with the reconstruction of our town. The damaged buildings, or what was left of them, had to be bulldozed and removed. Plans for rebuilding were in order. Hiring a new leader for the gas company was a priority, along with ebbing the community fears of another explosion. Thoughts of how to address the lawsuits that were certain to come were shelved but never far from the minds of the mayor and council. And there was the burying of the dead.

One funeral followed another, burial after burial. Sermons were preached on being prepared to meet the Redeemer. The children returned to school. Everyone searched for a return to normalcy. It would be some time before a routine returned to Villa Rica.

Human interest being what it is, we had reporters from the Atlanta papers—the *Journal* and the *Constitution*—looking for an inside story. John Billy, as a councilman and rescuer, received calls daily from those newspapers. He would recount the same story repeatedly, avoiding his personal participation in the rescue but praising the heroic efforts of those who risked their lives in the recovery efforts. He made it his purpose to commend the Negro citizens who came out to assist with the rescue efforts.

In 1957 Villa Rica was like most southern towns, segregated and bigoted. Even on Saturdays the downtown was devoid of any colored folks. An unwritten rule required the colored shoppers to steal away on the back streets to pick up their wares and groceries. I suppose that with the town coming together for the rescue efforts, both colored and white, John Billy had a realization of the humanity in all God's children.

Two weeks saw the funerals finalized but the mourning incomplete. Workers with heavy equipment had bulldozed and hauled the heart of the city off to an excavated pit near the school's football field.

Merchants and businessmen were again minding their concerns. The mayor and council hired a replacement to head the city's gas company.

John Billy came to me shortly after the new gasman had been found and hired. "The new gasman needs a place to live. The only place available right now is an old antiquated two-story house on North Avenue. I volunteered our house. It's just him, his wife, and their young daughter. They will rent from us, and we will rent the big house until they can find something permanent."

I thought again of Esther and "a time such as this". I made no protest, thinking it was God's will that we champion this cause for the good of our town.

The house on North Avenue was more than antiquated. It was haunting. John Billy said it had character. Johnny and Jody said it had characters living in the upstairs attic. And they constantly reminded the other three kids of the presence of our unseen lodgers.

The house had been unoccupied for some time but had last served as a boarding house, mostly for unmarried teachers from the school. I suppose at one time it would have been considered a manor house, but the Depression and war years had annulled its appeal and diminished its distinction. There were other homes nearby, family homes, that had stood the test of time. Our new home stood out like a shedding peacock's feather stuck in a fedora.

If indeed this house was haunted, then the haints must have been Siberians. With vaulted ceilings and expansive rooms, the house was bone-chillingly cold. The seven of us were, for that winter, forever clad in toboggans and woolen boot socks. Our potatoes and Campbell's soup cans froze solid in the pantry off from the kitchen. Noses ran like the falls at Slick Rock Creek. Our previous three homes in Villa Rica were summer cottages compared to the haunted house on North Avenue.

As was typical of northwest Georgia weather, the winters could run from middling to polar in a matter of days. That winter was no better or worse than any other winter, but in the big house, it was the coldest winter in my thirty-five years.

Eventually, the gasman found a brick home with heat not too far from the Baptist church. After he and his family cleared out, we were back into our now seemingly smaller mill house on Walker Street and back into our familial routines. Johnny and Jody, the seniors, and Sarah were high schoolers. Robert was going into the sixth grade and Darlene was a third grader. Our lives were centered on school and church activities—football, basketball, baseball, talent shows, dance recitals, Halloween festivals, Christmas pageants and Easter chorales.

Toward the end of the school year, I could sense that John Billy was again getting that itch to move on. I think he was waiting for Johnny and Jody to graduate, along with reasons enough to justify a relocation. The sparks for inducement to relocate began to build, but as usual, I was kept in the dark.

Though he never complained, I am certain the drive from Villa Rica to Marietta each night was wearing on him. It was a one-way distance of thirty miles, which meant he was on the road for nearly two hours each day. By week's end, he was exhausted from lack of sleep and trying to cram too much starch into the few daylight hours he had free.

After the town explosion, he became disillusioned and pessimistic with the small-town politics. Law suits started coming in over cause and responsibility, and doubtless the town was going to become bankrupt if the cause of action was upheld.

Other hostile challenges faced the city. Young men began to gather each Saturday night in the parking lot of a local eatery. Idle time and idle minds mixed with Budweiser led to devilment and troublemaking.

One young man was beaten within inches of his life. Highway 78 in front of the school was used as a racing strip with squalling tires and smoking engines. Citizens and businessmen lodged complaints, but the police were outmanned and bullied. After weeks of complaints about the troublemaking, the mayor and council, with the help of the Georgia State Patrol and Carroll County Sheriff's Office, coordinated a raid to round up the evildoers. Highway 78 and all other side exits were blocked to prevent escape. In all forty-two young men were arrested on charges of drunk driving, disorderly conduct, intent to incite a riot, destroying public property, and violation of the city's curfew.

The entire lot of young stallions was placed in the Villa Rica jail. Forty-two hellions in a jail designed to hold a handful of Saturday-night drunks and wife beaters did not meld. Within an hour of their incarceration, they destroyed the jail. Toilets and urinals were leveled to the floor. Windows were smashed save for the bars. Block walls were dismantled. Light fixtures were shattered. The state patrol and sheriff were alerted and summoned. They returned to transport the forty-two to the more secure county jail.

Not all the revelers were of the hoodlum stripe. Some just wanted to see fast cars, burning rubber, and street stunts. Others were curious onlookers who were without direction. Some were teens who wanted to drink a beer and take on the persona of Marlon Brando in *The Wild One*. Still and all, there were a few who were known transgressors with criminal records and bad reputations. The rest were just bootlickers looking for a good time. A handful, perhaps five, ended up doing time in the county jail, mostly for other offenses that were pending. The mass of the rabble were given stern warnings by a judge, blemishes on their records, and fines to cover the cost of the damage to the jail. The brag around town was that the hooligans vowed to be back the following weekend and bring their friends, but with the shepherds in jail, the sheep were put to pasture.

In time, the police department was severely criticized for allowing the delinquents to build to a crescendo of unruly rebellion. Images of *The Wild One* and *Blackboard Jungle* were, by 1958, carved into the collective consciousness of those who had survived the Great Depression and World War II. Villa Ricans were no different. The blame for the degeneracy of Villa Rica's youth fell inyo the laps of the police.

At the next monthly meeting of the city council, there was a flare-up over the resignation of the police chief. John Billy motioned at the council meeting that they accept the chief's resignation, and as timely as possible replace the entire six-man force. Tempers flared. Feelings were hurt. By the end of the council session, John Billy had resigned his position. The chains and burden of serving his city were lifted, and I think it was just another step toward emancipation from our current location.

The manifest of incentives to leave Villa Rica continued to mount. It was a city laboring in emotional and financial bankruptcy from the explosion. Minors were embracing major criminalities. And then there was the matter of John Billy's parents.

John Billy's pa was beginning to show signs of senility, and some of his lapses were becoming dangerous, not only to himself but to Miss Sarah as well. She caught him several times trying to kindle a morning fire in their gas heater. He would light newspaper and small wood chips before piling on the firewood.

It got worse. He insisted on driving his late '30s Ford to town each Friday for feed or seed, neither of which he had a need for.

For Mr. Bailey, finagling the columned gears became an act of woeful desperation. He could no longer remember the sequence of the shifts, and the clutch mechanics were long forgotten. Several townsmen had alerted John Billy that his pa was one clutch slip away from playing bumper cars with other shoppers. As much as they savored the spectacle of watching John Billy's pa reverse his way out of a parking space—the clamor of gears grinding and near misses of fender swipes—they, too, felt he was a danger to himself and to other motorists. Not only was he a menace on the road, but he also didn't know which road he was on. John Billy twice received calls from former neighbors when his pa was found at our old farm-place south of town. Once he was found at his old estate in Tallapoosa, gazing at the pasturing cows.

John Billy tried disconnecting his pa's battery, but oddly enough, on most days Mr. Bailey remembered that basic motor check and was able to crank his car. When disconnecting the battery cables failed to hamper Mr. Bailey's weekly motoring adventures, John Billy contrived a plan to forever uncouple his pa's dependency on his Ford. The ruse involved taking John Billy's pa on a masquerade surveying job at a friend's farm near Bowden Junction. Meanwhile, a second friend came in, removed the engine from Mr. Bailey's old Ford, and soldered the hood shut. Problem solved, one would think.

With the engineless Ford permanently parked, Mr. Bailey chose not to be bound by that annoying inconvenience. He started walking. He knew the direction of Villa Rica from his home but could never seem to find the town. The three-mile walk to town had too many diversions. Mr. Bailey was becoming Sybil the Uncivil and Tickle Pink—a town fixture to be patronized by the hoi polloi. He was becoming my ma in her slumbering years.

John Billy now felt a solitary responsibility for his parents. His rather large family was scattered from Florida to Ohio to Germany to Kwajalein in the Pacific. None of his family members were near Villa Rica to offer aid and comfort. It was a responsibility he took on but never embraced.

Miss Sarah was of a sharp mind but did not have the physical capability to grapple with the demands of Mr. Bailey when he was on the move. However, in a short time, he began to roam less as his body strength began to taper.

Johnny and Jody graduated in the spring and by fall were enrolled at West Georgia College in Carrollton. Both were maintaining their jobs. Berry Pharmacy had rebuilt and reopened, so Johnny was still part time there, and Jody was still at the EZ Shop. After three quarters of college life, both boys felt it was time to get a nine-to-five. A call to a cousin in Atlanta resulted in both boys latching on with the Sears and Roebuck distribution center on Jefferson Street in Atlanta. Together they purchased a Volkswagen bug and began to make the trek to Atlanta each day.

John Billy knew well the grind of making a long-distance drive east from Villa Rica along US 78, or at least this gave him another motive for moving closer not only his work but to their's as well. After six months, we were on the move again.

Miss Sarah and John Billy decided that the best thing for Mr. Bailey was to move him from their large honeybee infested home to a smaller place. Our home on Walker Street was sold to Miss Sarah and Mr. Bailey, while my kids and I were uprooted from our home once again. Our new hometown post address was in the unfamiliar clime of Austell, Georgia.

As with all our previous moves, my first glimpse of our new home was on moving day. As was John Billy's wont, he selected the house and the locale. Not quite in a neighborhood, the house was located along the Austell-Marietta Road—it was one of many saltbox houses harboring Lockheed workers.

The only positive I could garner was that this would be our first house of brick masonry. It was still too small for our large family. It was a two-bedroom, one-bath with a pine-paneled den that was recast into a bedroom for the boys. But John Billy had plans for expansion.

The house sat on almost half a basement foundation, which consisted mostly of dirt and spiders and a horde of camelback crickets.

"We will dig out the basement and put the boys' bedroom down there," he said.

"I'll stock up on calamine lotion for the insect bites. I'll probably need to buy a snakebite kit as well," I responded with impudence.

"It'll have walls and a ceiling. We can use Black Flag to kill any bugs," he responded.

"I'll write Talmage to see if he has any surplus gas masks from the war," I said with even more sass.

Of course, there was no dissuading John Billy once he set his mind to something. When Jody was temporarily laid off from Sears and Roebucks the digging began. Jody and John Billy, but mostly Jody since he was home all day, worked the pick-axes and shovels, chipping away at the dirt wall, while Robert was assigned the wheelbarrow to dump the dirt in a low spot in our back yard.

Since the only entrance to the basement was from the backyard, I asked John Billy, "Are the boys going to have to go outside again to go to bed?"

"No," he said. "I'm going to use the hall closet. We'll knock out the floor and build steps down to their bedroom."

"You are going to destroy a perfectly good closet to build stairs? We don't have enough closet space as it is, and that's the only space we have for the kids' and our winter jackets. Isn't there another way to get to the basement?" I asked.

"Well, you don't want them going outside. I thought about a fireman's pole, but that is only a one-way trip. They would have to come back up to the main floor from the outside. I could build a grand staircase in the living room, but then we would have no living room. This will work. You'll see."

John Billy left the closet rod and hanging jackets in what was once a hall closet. The boys had to part the winter jackets to descend or ascend to and from their bedroom. John Billy didn't bother installing heat. His reasoning, he said, was that the basement would be like a cave with a steady temperature—not too hot or too cool. On that he was correct. Like a cave, it was the perfect medium for spiders and camel-backs.

AUSTELL, GEORGIA: 1960-2015

I Move, Therefore I Am

The riddle for me was that I couldn't fathom whether John Billy was moving toward something or running away from something. I knew his pa's history was one of moving on to the next farm—looking for bigger, better ground with more production. However, he never seemed to find his promised land. He, like Moses, was bound to Moab.

John Billy, on the other hand, started running as a young man when his pa chased him off his farm with a sling of rocks for eating biscuits and jelly before his chores were complete. Just as he went back to his pa's farm to work until he was old enough to leave for good, he repeated that pattern when he ferried me from the white sands of Charleston to the red clay of Georgia. It seemed I was caught up in an ecclesiastical recurrence of moving from place to place—what was before will be again; there is no new thing under the sun.

Perhaps John Billy's brothers found their own way to keep moving. Both being career military men, Talmage in the army and air force and Paul in the navy, they were never in one place for very long. The war took them both far away to the Pacific theater, and the postwar years stationed them from the Great Lakes to Hawaii to Pensacola for one and from Savannah to Germany to Arizona for the other.

John Billy's relocation syndrome—or should I say dislocation syndrome?—did not cease with our move to Austell. In fact, it waxed into a search for his own personal contentment for his definition of success. Like his father, he kept looking for the bigger, the better—a proof of a life not squandered.

In the decade of 1960s, we made seven moves, all but one within a radius of five miles of one another. The first move was no less than fifty yards behind our original home in Austell. The backyards butted against each other. A new subdivision drew John Billy's attention, a deal was made and we were on the move. This second home was complete with a full basement with prebuilt stairs that were not closeted with a curtain of jackets.

Five years passing saw five children leave home. Johnny, Sarah, and Darlene were married and Jody joined the Marine Corps. Robert was now a student at West Georgia College and was only home on weekends. That was a cue for John Billy to downsize and possibly make a profit from the current home. The house was sold, and we moved into a rental about a half mile away. Meanwhile, John Billy searched for his next mini-manse.

The next selection was a first for us, a home with central airconditioning and heat. It was very likely over our budget, and I knew we would not be there long. Once Robert graduated from West Georgia, a move was inevitable. Next stop was a rental on a foreboding street named Black Boulevard. The boulevard was an aging, potholed cul-de-sac no more than four miles from the previous home.

Next on the dislocation docket was a shift from John Billy's norm of moving a rock-throwing distance from our previous home. Lockheed was looking for a live-in caretaker for the company's campgrounds on Lake Lanier, about a two-hour drive north from Austell. John Billy applied for the position, but never bothered to share that bit of information with me until he was selected and we were on the move again.

I resented this move more than any other—more so even than our move from Charleston to the bedeviled red clay farm in Villa Rica. My kids were grown and starting their families. So not only was I being sundered from my children, I was to be absent from the blossoming of my grandchildren.

Each day on the lake became a day of more and more isolation. In the summer months, from sunup to sundown John Billy was tending the camp grounds—registering guests, picking up garbage, maintaining the grounds, repairing boats and motors, and schmoozing with the campers. In the dead of winter, there was less for John Billy to do, but he found a way to do it anyway. All the while my role was to prepare his meals, watch daytime TV, and ponder my yesterdays. Between *The Today Show*, *Hollywood Squares* and *Search for Tomorrow*, *As the World Turns*, and *The Guiding Light*, I was either cooking or cleaning.

My realization was that my life was one of cloistered isolation. I had no lifelong friends. After years in the Catholic orphanage, I could not tell you the name of one of the misbegotten paupers who shared that reformatory aside from my own sister. After the orphanage, I was insulated on an island with an outraged, bitter old crippled pa and a moonstruck ma. Immediately after I married John Billy, my life and time were consumed with birthing and raising babies. Six sucklings in ten years left little time for everlasting sisterhood.

John Billy's being constantly on the move and my inability to drive a car only meant more isolation. I once asked him to teach me to drive. His response was "Why do you need to drive? I can take you anywhere you need to go."

The only places he ever took me were places where he wanted to go. While on the farm, he had no time to go anywhere. It was Lockheed, farming, and sleep with an occasional Sunday visit to his ma's and pa's or to his sister's place in Tallapoosa.

I came to realize that my life was defined by place. My time markers were about a homeplace, fused with memories of a field, a yard, a house, a room, a child. Aside from my own family, people were a supplement—yes, at times a complement, but never central to the telling of my story. My fiction of place was one of generational birth and death, of children growing up and adults dying. My fantasy of place had a foothold in forever. But those illusions were not to be. My footing was forever on a tottering tract. No sooner was I on stable ground than the bedrock was splintered asunder. The firmness of the sands of Sullivan's Island shifted. The firmness of the red clay of our Georgia farm eroded.

I think the spirit of place could be strong, if it were lasting, but it is hard to know who you are until you know where you are. Moving as we did left us without a sense of history, and of course, geography. This unstable foundation left me, and dare I say my family, with an ever-sentimental mood of homesickness.

I suppose we all have the weight of generational history in the cores of our being. I have uncounted generations of Irish blood in my peculiar mix, and those spans of Irish natives, my forefathers and mothers, believed in family, community, and love of Irish heritage.

Circumstances with the potato forced an uprooting of the Irish, with many settling in Charleston. I was of the third generation of that Charleston-Irish coupling. That's almost one hundred years of supported family and friends—and most importantly, one hundred years of ties to one place. Dare I say that my Irish sense of home and stability was suspect of John Billy's nomadic ramblings? His people were pilgrims to Virginia. Then it was a migration to North Carolina, South Carolina, east Georgia, west Georgia, and Alabama. They couldn't keep still.

Two years on Lake Lanier was enough. I had forged a single friendship with a German lady, a World War II war bride who was living on the lake with her husband, not far from the Lockheed campground. Since I could not drive, I only visited her when John Billy had nothing else to do at the campground, which was generally in the wintertime. Our time together was spent with her telling tales of Hitler's Germany and teaching me the art of knitting. However, that neighborliness was not strong enough to hobble me to the waters of Lake Lanier. When John Billy suggested that we might move back to be near my kids, I praised God and packed my bags.

As I knew he would, John Billy grew weary of the rote monotony of being a campground maintenance man and director. The enthusiasm of living on the lake waned by the end of the first year. The month of December saw us moving back to Austell to within a mile and a half of the first home we had purchased ten years earlier and within a few miles of all of my children.

This was our final move: a full circle, as it were. The mystery of some kind of mathematical muddling of pi—we moved once every 3.14159 years. We were back to another squared cracker box of four rooms and a privy pot. As at all of our homes, John Billy had his garden. His life was incomplete without produce. My life was simply incomplete.

I had been voiceless and powerless for over seventy years. To John Billy, I was just another of his six kids, a menial attendant there to do his bidding. Each evening for thirty years, I laid out his fireman's uniform for work. On Sundays I laid out his dress pants, coat, and tie for church. When he was watching TV, if he needed a smoke, it was "Get me a cigarette." If he was thirsty, "Get me a glass of water." I followed the dictates without question, even lighting the cigarettes.

I was housebound and indentured for life. Any escape from one of the uncountable houses we called home was restricted to the whims of John Billy. Vacations were never family adventures, nor were they a respite from the tedium of attending to John Billy's demands. His vocabulary was simple—"Fetch…," "Bring me…'" "Get me…," "Do this…," "Do that…." A trained bird dog could have served his purpose if they had the ability to cook and light a cigarette.

I suppose I was schooled in the art of obedience from an early age. I goosed-stepped behind Sis down every avenue of endangerment she could muster. The nuns permitted nothing less than strict subordination. And my pa was a tyrant, at least in the confines of his own home. The craft of capitulation was mine to own, and I owned it well.

However, I did have a saving grace from the curbs and limits on my free will. That, of course, was my children. They were mine to raise for the most part. Up to the time they were grown and gone, I was their defender, their buffer, their harbor, and their rescuer. For thirty years that was my purpose, but with the kids cleared out, I was in a place of singular seclusion, segregated to a world befitting John Billy's arbitrary dictates.

Outside of weekend excursions with my girls, grocery shopping with John Billy, and an occasional Florida visit to visit a brother or to fish, I was chained to the same routine I had been bound to all my life with the exception of tending to youngsters' needs. While John Billy piddled in his garden from sunup to supper, I was again housebound with soaps and game shows and cooking three squares a day—followed by a dish wash, wipe, and put away. My house was spotless, and why should it not be? All I had was idle time.

One would think that time would be stagnant during the alleged golden years, but the years moved right along, not waiting for me or John Billy. We never thought much or said much about the inevitable. The seasons were surging past, and the winters seemed to fight endlessly against the spring's rally. And so it was with John Billy's winter wilting.

For as long as I could remember, John Billy awoke each morning with a phlegmy glob of throat mucus that he couldn't quite bring up from the depths of his esophagus. His guttural gravels had no melody. They were jarring and strained. I tried to add levity with "Can I get you another cigarette?"

At the end, my flippancy had lost its sway in convincing him that his smoking was going to kill him. Over the years, as the foreboding cough became more frequent, John Billy switched from unfiltered Camels, trying several filtered brands to no avail. The bearish hacks worsened in the passing years.

John Billy was diagnosed with inoperable esophageal cancer. It was at this time that he decided that he needed to give up the habit. When asked by an oncologist if he smoked, his reply was "no". Sarah, who had accompanied him to the doctor, stepped in "Daddy, you stopped five days ago."

"Well, I quit, didn't I?" was his response. The doctor smiled.

It was in the fading months after his diagnosis that he attempted to prepare me for life as an independent woman. Learning to drive a car was out of the question at my age of sixty-four but I needed to learn how to handle the everyday responsibilities that he had commanded from the day of our marriage in Charleston.

"OK," he said one evening after he came in from picking his early tomatoes and young squash. "I am going to show you how to balance the checkbook."

"Shouldn't you have done that fifty years ago?" I asked, with sass.

He ignored me as he laid out the bills for the month on the kitchen table.

"The first thing you do is enter your deposits," he said.

"What deposits?" I asked.

"Your income."

"I don't have an income," I protested.

"Yes, you do. You get Social Security, and I have my retirement from Lockheed and my Social Security," he explained.

"I get your Social Security and your retirement check? I wish I had known that years ago," I said, again with a whisper of more sass.

"Well, no. I think you get a burial fee from Social Security, but the retirement check ends when I die. We set up the retirement so that we had more money coming in for retirement while we were living and less later on," he said, reasoning to himself more than explaining to me.

"Don't you mean you set up the retirement that way? I don't remember us discussing that at all. And I think zero is a lot less than what you are bringing in now."

I knew his thinking. His plan—no his expectation—was that he would live long after I had passed.

"How much will Social Security pay toward your burial?" I asked.

"I'm not sure. I will have to look that up. It is in the folder," he said, itching to move on to the finer art of check balancing.

"Do we have any life insurance?" I asked. I remembered a Mr. Elkins used to come by regularly to collect a few dollars toward a life policy, but I had no idea if it was ever paid up.

"We have a couple of policies. They are in the folder," he said. "I will have to look them up."

The folder was a simple cardboard accordion pouch where we kept all of our important papers—car titles, mortgage paperwork, loan payments for his Troy-Built tractor, and presumably stacks of life policies and Social Security guarantees for a decent burial. Not that any of this mattered. We never got around to organizing the folder, nor did we ever look anything up before his passing.

"We can do all that later. Let's focus on balancing the checkbook," he said, bringing me back to the table full of bills.

"OK, at the first of the month, you enter your deposits here in this column," he said as he wrote in the amounts from his retirement check and the two Social Security checks. "Then you start entering your withdrawals. That's the bills you are paying."

He then began to write checks for the bill payments. Without comment, he wrote bill after bill and entered each payment in his register. After a spell of following his entries, I noticed that he was not writing in the same amount that he had entered on the check for payment.

"That bill for the tractor payment was $127.80," I interrupted. "You only entered $125.00".

"That's my secret stash," he explained. "That is how I build up my account. I always have more in my account than the register shows——my little nest egg for emergencies."

"I thought this was a demonstration of how to balance a checkbook. Where does the balancing part come in?"

He ignored me.

"Wouldn't it have been better if you had allowed me to write the checks and enter the amounts in the columns?" I asked.

"That would have taken too long," he said as he put away his checkbook. "Don't worry, the kids will help you do all that."

So much for being prepared for life after his passing, but he was correct. The independence I gained from John Billy's passing became absolute dependence on my children. There were no short trips for errands without a son or daughter providing transportation. Grocery shopping became a family affair with me tagging along. I did learn to keep my checkbook, but I had to have one of my kids check the balance at the end of the month.

John Billy's passing went kindly smooth, with little difficulty or pain. As the cancer grew, his oxygen levels began to decline. Eventually he was hospitalized, but there was nothing they could do except keep him as comfortable as possible. He was strong up to the end, with no complaints aside from saying "I can't breathe."—his dying words.

Jody had moved into the spare bedroom in the months before John Billy's passing to help me tend to him. After the funeral he stayed on for support, but the kids decided that selling my home was best for me in that I could use the money from the sale to bolster my portfolio. I had never had a portfolio before, but I did understand that I needed mine bolstered now that I had one. John Billy did leave me three life insurance policies of $1,500, $650, and $250 and with the $250 I received from Social Security I was almost able to bury him the full six feet under. The kids chipped in for the remainder, but there was nothing left for my newly acquired portfolio.

The house sold quickly with some profit, and I was on the move again. This time, I settled in Darlene's basement apartment. It was cozy enough, with a bedroom-living room combo and a kitchenette off to the wing. It was nothing extravagant, but it served its purpose and it was home.

Facing the prospect of death in old age leaves one with a mixed bag of tempers. There is, of course, the denial. I wasn't ready to leave my children and grands. I had lived my life, but I wanted to witness their stories as they continued to hammer through their own sagas. I wanted to be a witness—to see their stories unfold. I wanted happily-ever-after endings for them all.

I dealt with guilt, depression, and anger. The guilt was no more than second-guessing—Monday-morning quarter-backing my boys would call it. Could I have done better—been a better wife, been a better mother, been a better person? I was satisfied that I had, under the circumstances, been the best that I could be.

My depression was short lived. My children didn't allow me an opening for self-pitying blues. An idle mind being the devil's workshop, my children didn't provide Satan the tools to set up his smithery. They kept me busy. I was the focus of every family get-together and there was never a feeling of being a burden to anyone.

Dealing with my anger was altogether another knot to be untangled. John Billy was the source of my anger, but of course, there was nothing I could do about it after his passing. I was angry at myself because of my inability to stand up for myself, for being the pacifier.

Nevertheless, life moved on. The focus moved to frogs and tadpoles—my children and their little angels. I oft repeated my tales, from Charleston and the Catholic orphanage, to the hurly-burly of the red clay farm in Georgia in hopes that they would all remember a heritage with heart and soul.

Epilogue

None could fathom that my Mom would live another thirty years after the passing of my Dad. While her mind was still sound, I and my brothers and sisters took her home to Charleston for one final visit. But Mama could never return to Charleston, not in any real and meaningful way.

Charleston was the place of her birth. It was the place where she sprouted, where she flowered. Believe me, it is still her home, her roots, but she could never go back there. She had been gone from Charleston for near sixty years. Now it is her rickety memory and shaky senses, feeble as they are, that keep her memory of Charleston alive. Sadly, that life is ending. Five years of retirement village and now, ten days of intensive care as her kidney's fail her.

Sometimes Mama thinks she can see Charleston, but the Charleston she sees is faint—a Depression-era Charleston, not the Charleston she hears about today, full of rich tourist and uppity Yankees who like fancy dancing and classical music.

Sometimes Mama thinks she can hear Charleston, but the truth of the matter is she doesn't hear much of anything anymore. Her hearing left years ago. Screaming became our means of communication with her, yet even with the shouting, most conversation was misunderstood.

"HOW'S YOUR INGROWN TOENAIL?" I might shout. "No, I didn't get any mail."

"DID THE PREACHER VISIT?" "What creature is it?"

Mama wouldn't want to touch the Charleston she knew. What she remembers of Charleston is a dirty, crumbly old sea town, but mama sure would love to smell her again. Some people say Charleston stinks, but Mama doesn't remember that. She once said, "It is kinda like when you let one slip and everybody gets up and runs and hoots and hollers, but you don't mind the smell because it's your own. Sure, it don't smell like Aunt Katie's rose garden, but it ain't nothing to make a stink about either. And if you sit there long enough, you'll get used to it just like I got used to the smells of Charleston."

About the only good sense Mama has left is on her tongue, and, boy would she love to taste Charleston again—the crabs and the shrimps and rice.

"They don't eat like us in Georgia," she once said. Mama had been living in Georgia since 1952. Mama summed up her view of Georgia cuisine this way: "In Georgia they get stuck on a food and they see how many ways they can ruin it. Take corn, for example. They eat it fried, boiled, baked, creamed, grated, grilled, breaded, poned, and gritted. They especially like it gritted but don't have enough God-given sense to fix it with shrimps. Georgia crackers do the same thing with potatoes. They fry 'em, patty 'em, mash 'em, salad 'em, chip 'em, and bake 'em. I guess in some ways you have to admire Georgians when it comes to their eating. They don't give up on a food if they hate it; they just find another way to defeat it."

Yes, Mama grew up right there in Charleston, right where the Cooper and Ashley rivers, as all Charlestonians like to brag, "come together to fill up the Atlantic Ocean." Mama couldn't tell them apart. The Cooper smelled like the Ashley, the Ashley smelled like the Cooper, and they both smelled like the Atlantic. It made no difference to her. Mama knew it was Charleston's smell, and it smelled good to her—not like Savannah.

She went to Savannah once to visit Uncle Talmage and Aunt Jerry. "It stunk," she said, drifting off on another avenue. "It smelled like my pa's room when he was dying. You didn't want to go back there once you left. I mean—I never wanted to go back to Savannah. I did go back to my pa's room. He was dying, and it was my responsibility to tend to him. Looking back on things, I think my pa was dying all his life."

My mama, like her pa, probably spent her life dying too, but she was unaware. Perhaps we are all unaware.

About the Author

Robert Bailey and his four siblings were born on Sullivan's Island, South Carolina, then transplanted to Villa Rica, Georgia. After earning his BA, MEd, and EdS, he worked for many years as a high school teacher and soccer coach. He taught advanced placement American government, psychology, philosophy, and comparative religion, and was also certified as an ESL and Gifted and Talented teacher. In 1976 he was named the Georgia Coach of the Year, and was recently inducted into his school's Athletic Hall of Fame.

During the 1980s he wrote an observational humor column for a weekly newspaper in Rabun County, Georgia, and is currently working as a personal fitness trainer at a local gym. After retirement, he spent three years at Mercer University supervising prospective teachers.

Robert married his 8th grade sweetheart, and they have been married 53 years.

Lightning Source UK Ltd.
Milton Keynes UK
UKHW021024251122
412794UK00014B/1598